Allan R. Mendelsohn

THE WORK OF SOCIAL WORK

New Viewpoints
A Division of Franklin Watts
New York/London

New Viewpoints
A Division of Franklin Watts
730 Fifth Avenue
New York, New York 10019

Library of Congress Cataloging in Publication Data

Mendelsohn, Allan R
    The work of social work.

    Bibliography: p.
    Includes index.
    1. Social service. I. Title.
HV40.M483   361.3   79-25462
ISBN 0-531-05412-8
ISBN 0-531-05626-0 pbk.

CONTENTS

Five

UNDERSTANDING OTHERS—COMMUNICATION

Six

THE INTERACTION

THE
WORK
OF
SOCIAL
WORK

ONE

SOCIAL WORK— THE ACTIVE PROFESSION

The roots of social work reach deep into Judeo-Christian history. Reflecting an abiding interest in the nature and values of people, of how they live and struggle to survive within the social environment, the profession of social work, until recently, has been directed toward only those members of society who seemingly have less than others, are not able to fully participate in society, and need assistance in order to deal more productively with their life and times. The traditional concern of social work has been with the neglected, the underdog.

Today, however, the practice of social work has been broadened to include *all* members of society in recognition of the complexity of contemporary industrialized society in which everyone, at one time or another, needs assistance to adequately negotiate its systems. In response to this recognition, social work has moved toward providing a broader range of service to more people than the traditionally defined "underprivileged." The current goal of social work to "advance the quality of life" reflects these more universal concerns and implies the advancement of *all* life. The manner by which social work goes about its task of advancing the quality of life is the subject of this book.

The nature of social work's mission, its history, and its values make a comprehensive definition of social work difficult to elucidate. Its definition by the public is often confused; its definition of itself undergoes continual change. The public image of the social worker reflects a wide range of possibilities, from a bomb-throwing revolutionary at one end of the scale to a thoughtful scholar at the other. Perhaps equally divergent are the images that social workers have of themselves, a "psychiatric" social worker at one end of the scale and a "concrete service deliverer" at the other.

The confusion regarding the "image" of social work arises from the nature of social work itself as an *active* profession whose virtue lies in its versatility. What social workers do at any particular time depends on the particular circumstances of the situation and the extent of their involvement. For example, a social worker sitting in a pleasantly furnished office speaking with a neatly dressed husband and wife presents a picture not unlike that conveyed by a psychologist, a psychiatrist, or a clergyman. Or, working in a school situation, the social worker may, at times, be perceived as an educator and may actually be performing an educative function. In other situations social workers might appear to be parent surrogates, law enforcement officers, recreation leaders, and so on.

Because it is an active profession, social work can be defined more precisely by considering not *what* social work does but *how*.

ADVANCING THE QUALITY OF LIFE

The grandiose gesture of advancing the quality of life relates to man's continuing attempts to improve his life in a complex, industrialized society, a society marked by a glut of material manufacture, a systematic imbalance in the allocation of resources, and a persistent psychological pressure. This broad and quixotic mission has been mandated by society, and the profession, for its part, has accepted the challenge.

Its mission is further confounded, however, in that the quality of life that the profession is dedicated to advancing is itself a constantly changing dynamic, an ongoing process with no discernible end. What may be considered an "acceptable" quality of life at one given time and place may not be acceptable in another. Social work must constantly reevaluate itself, its purpose, and its mission, for conditions change, times change, values change, and social work's goals must reflect those changes.

To get at the nuts and bolts of the "quality of life," the phrase must be broken down into more meaningful entities, into the specifics of housing, clothing, sustenance, and physical, financial, and emotional well-being, all of which must be viewed in contemporary terms and reflect the reality of this place and this time. To improve the quality of life, social work must be cognizant of what resources are available as well as the best allocation of those resources. It cannot afford to lock itself into frozen postures of service. The social and psychological needs of people are not static.

As the quality of life is redefined in a changing psychosocial landscape, the demand for social services increases and responses to those demands become more and more refined. Services, in other words, have become more specialized, and the growing complexity of the service delivery system has created a need for experts to inform the consumer of not only the wide variety of services available but also how to gain access to those services. Indeed, the complexity of contemporary life and the service delivery networks has forced social workers themselves to seek help in negotiating the pathways. Because of this burgeoning specialization, survival has become increasingly difficult, for the distance between the service provider and the service receiver has widened.

The increasing confusion experienced by the consumer in gaining access to the proliferation of offered services has prompted steps to lessen the difficulty. Large institutions are decentralizing, or "unitizing" (smaller, more manageable units within the institutional structure, that is, little institutions within bigger institutions). Through smaller units, social services are being reintroduced into the community, offering visibility to community populations and simplified access routes. Along with community-based services, multiservice approaches are being developed. A variety of services are being offered under one roof. Mutual help groups are being developed; teams of professionals of different disciplines, paraprofessionals, consumers, members of the community power structures, all are working together to resolve issues of common concern. As these visible and accessible service modules develop, the distance between service providers and service receivers correspondingly lessens and the pursuit of an improved quality of life is thus more viable.

SOCIAL WELFARE—SOCIAL WORK: A DISTINCTION

Although the terms "social welfare" and "social work" are frequently confused and consequently used interchangeably, their meanings are not the same.

Social meaning "having to do with people living together in a situation requiring that they have dealings with one another" and *welfare* "being the state of being or doing well; conditions of health, happiness and prosperity," "social welfare" is a term applied to the broad spectrum of "social" services designed to meet the "welfare" needs of human beings that are "recognized as basic to the well-being of the population and the better functioning of the social order." Included under the social welfare umbrella is a veritable army of both public and private service-oriented professions—teaching, medicine, counseling, nursing, psychological counseling, occupational therapy, paraprofessional services, jurisprudence, and *social work*—operating for the commonweal. So, the term "social work" is applied to but one profession, albeit a unique profession, among many designed to meet the needs of people interacting with one another and to provide a condition of prosperity that reflects the basic interests of the population and the social order. The concept of social welfare is constantly changing as the social conditions of society change and new social realities emerge.

A CLIENT, A PATIENT,
OR A CONSUMER?

Until recently, the word "client" was used to describe recipients of social services. According to Webster, a client is: "one leaning on another 1. in ancient Rome, a plebian who was dependent on a patrician patron 2. a dependent person under the patronage of another 3. a person or company in its relationship to a lawyer, accountant, etc., engaged to act in its behalf 4. loosely, a customer."

The first two definitions, indicating dependency, refer, in a raw sense, to the powerlessness of the "client." In the social work sense, the "client" is seemingly powerless in relationship to the social worker who is seemingly powerful. In the early history of social work, the "client" was indeed seen as powerless, as the dependent and needful person. The early dispensers of service saw themselves as patrons; as beneficent, righteous, all good and worthy, possessed of the finer attributes and resources, which they chose to bestow on the less fortunate. This sense of Lady (eventually Lord) Bountiful gave way, during the professionalization of the field, to the third and fourth definitions, which stress a lessening of the distance between the dispenser and the receiver of service. A social worker is now "engaged" to act on another's behalf; the "client" becomes a "customer," a selector of service.

With the emphasis on psychological service and the use of a medical model for social work practice, the "client" became the "patient" and is still referred to as "patient" by social workers in hospitals and other medical settings. The term "patient" in this sense refers to persons who have something "wrong" with themselves. Patients in this social work setting are to be "cured" of something, a throwback to the earlier definition of the powerless "client." Both the earlier word "client" and later word "patient" implied a basic fault (moral or physical) in the service receiver.

Recent social work literature has raised serious questions about the use of the "medical" model. The recognition of social, economic, geographical, catastrophic, familial, and financial causative factors, as well as internal physiological and psychological factors, has prompted a shift from the medical model. To reflect the changing attitudes toward those who receive social services, a different term, "the consumer," has been introduced.

The term "consumer" presupposes rights to services as well as needs for services. An attempt to redefine the giving/receiving equation, the term "consumer" underscores the mutually respectful, transactional nature of professional relationships. As everyone is a consumer, the new concept is erasing the fine line between those "in need" and those "not in need," between "clients" and "nonclients," between "patient" and "doctor" and broadening the profession of social work to extend its services to not just the poor but to *all* consumers.

SOCIAL WORK SANCTION

The profession of social work cannot depend solely upon a time or a place or even a political leadership in order to identify social needs and the most appropriate ways to meet them. As nothing more than a political instrument, social work could neither lay claim to any semblance of professionalism nor could it remain faithful to its own value system. Yet social work does recognize its participation in a sociopolitical structure and that its continued existence depends on the financial support of that structure. Consequently, the scope of the profession is influenced by the sociopolitical milieu, and that milieu must, in turn, be influenced by the profession. It is in the give-and-take battleground between the dictates of the sociopolitical milieu and the recognized needs of people that social work has been most effective. It struggles, on the one hand, to influence the sociopolitical structure under which people live and, on the other, to help people to come to the most advantageous terms with the existing social realities. Thus, social work recognizes both the right of society to *sanction* its practice and the rights of people that must be protected by the profession's adherence to a system of *values*.

Social work is generally accomplished within the boundaries of an "agency," an institutional organization designed to meet identified social needs. It is this organization that sanctions, or permits, the work performed by social workers (workers in private practice are sanctioned only by their academic degrees). The agency itself is sanctioned by a board of directors and/or government regulatory agencies, which, through financing and approvals, permit the agency to function within established limits. The acceptance of sanctioning by the profession represents its acknowledgment of its accountability to society.

The system of values upon which social work is predicated reflects its commitment to, and respect for, people. The value system contains the following self-imposed limits to protect people even from those who would offer service.

- The concept of *self-determination* ensures that the basic right of people to make their own decisions about their own lives to the maximum possible extent will not be subverted, that is, the individual's right to make decisions is protected even if such decisions are contrary to the prevailing norms.

● The concept of the *dignity of the individual* ensures that basic respect and dignity will be accorded all people in their dealings with social workers regardless of the conditions, situations, or problems, that is, the individual is protected from being shamed, for example, by the social worker into conforming to accepted social behavior.

● The concept of the *confidentiality of communication* ensures that the right to privacy will be maintained in all interactions with social workers, that is, "seditious" thoughts or "alien" feelings shared by the individual with the social worker, for example, will not casually be disclosed to the authorities. Social workers do not yet enjoy the "privileged" communication as exists between doctor and patient, lawyer and client or priest and parishioner. Confidentiality is the closest substitute.

Thus, despite social work's sanction by social authority, this value system ensures that the rights of the individual will not be corrupted by either the prevailing social philosophy or social workers themselves. The value system will be discussed further in Chapter Two.

SOCIAL WORK AS PRACTICE

The term "social work" is considered by some an unfortunate choice. It lacks professionalism. The title "social worker" appears to them to lack the professional patina of the more prestigious professions, such as medicine and law, for example, where the workers don't "work," they "practice." Social workers are doomed "to work," however, for attempts to introduce new titles, such as social engineer, change agent, and social therapist, have failed, and the designation of social worker has persisted, a constant reminder of the profession's commitment to work to meet the needs of people.

As a "practice," social work demands a performance, the provision of services to persons in need. To accomplish this end, the worker must deal with an incredibly complex human being who defies prediction. Even though social work's already considerable knowledge is constantly being reevaluated as well as increased, the social theory it propounds nevertheless remains inexact. Human behavior, consequently, cannot be accurately predicted simply because not enough is yet known about what makes people behave the way they do in various environmental situations. The needs of people, however, demand attention here and now; their needs cannot wait until knowledge reaches scientific accuracy. The action needed reflects the conditions of the present; social workers in practice must, therefore, use the knowledge and techniques that are available at that moment in time. They must make the best guesses possible under these conditions. Often certainty remains elusive, but the practice of social work cannot afford the luxury of delay, for the needs are often too pressing to tarry.

Despite significant changes in social work procedure, the value base of social work—self-determination, the dignity of the individual, and confidentiality—has withstood the ideological changes of society and remained constant since social work evolved from a well-intentioned service to a disciplined profession.

Social-work practice reveals the two-sided nature of its professional charge. On the one hand, it is committed to people who are in need of service now. On the other, it contains a commitment to better those systems and institutions that significantly affect how man lives together with his fellow, that is, the social, economic, and political structures that govern formalized relationships. In other words, social work practice is concerned with both helping people in need now and alleviating the societal factors that cause the need. Historically, however, social work's most effective performance has been in providing direct human services; its performance in the area of social change, unfortunately, has been less effective. This dichotomy has resulted, perhaps, because of limited resources that further aggravate the situation by dividing the two sides of the charge connected by ''and'' into an either/or argument. Regardless of one's position in the continuing debate, however, it is nevertheless obvious that one without the other is unacceptable. A social worker involved in effecting change in welfare laws also recognizes the need for money now, not at some eventual time when the law is changed. When verifying the eligibility of a welfare recipient, the worker also recognizes that the complex and dehumanizing procedures through which help is granted are in need of change.

Today's world, eclectic and ever-changing, demands that man adapt or perish. As the postindustrial social environment becomes more and more complex, it is increasingly evident that *all* people, not only the underprivileged, need help in coping, in adapting, at one time or another, and therein lies the raison d'être of social work.

The necessary adaptations reflect the dynamics of the existing realities and values of a given time. In contemporary society an appropriate survival kit is somewhat more substantial than that considered adequate in an earlier day. To give a child of the seventies just enough to survive—just enough food to avoid starvation, just enough shelter, just enough clothing—verges on negligence. Yet in another time, in a time when people died of starvation, such a survival kit would have been considered exceedingly humane.

The concept of advancing the quality of life has introduced

other values that go beyond mere physical survival; such concepts as self-fulfillment, enjoyment, satisfaction, and human potential are advanced. The transition from a society of scarcity to a society of abundance has produced the irony that for the first time in history more people die of overeating than of starvation. However, just how far society is willing to go beyond meeting the sheer survival needs of its members and how much impact social work will have in setting new priorities and goals has yet to be determined.

FIELDS OF PRACTICE

Social work is concerned with almost all situations where people interact with both other people and social institutions. The wide range of social work includes practice in the following areas:

- *Child Welfare.* Working with children to provide foster care, adoption services, institutional care, preventive services, protective services, and family counseling.
- *Public Assistance.* Working with people receiving assistance (usually financial) from the state; verification of eligibility, concrete service provision, employment counseling, need assessment, and so on. (Departments of Welfare generally provide a wide range of services, which will be identified under functional headings. Many child-welfare services, for example, can be included under a public assistance heading.)
- *Health Care and Services.* Working in hospitals, clinics, comprehensive health care centers, and primary care facilities, where the basic service is medical; the social worker assists the medical staff in meeting the social needs of the patients.
- *Corrections.* Working with offenders in a court setting or in prison settings, detention centers, youth houses, and training

centers, where social behavior is the prime consideration, and providing probationary or parole services.

- *School Services.* Working in a school setting, with students and families, teachers and administrators, where education is the prime factor.
- *Aging.* Working with the elderly in a variety of settings—the community, old-age residences, nursing homes, health-related facilities, Golden Age clubs, Gray Panthers—where the problems of growing old in contemporary society are primary.
- *International Services.* Dealing with social problems between nations and with the international issues of poverty and immigration under the auspices of the United Nations and UNNRA.
- *Industrial Services.* Working with unions and management to resolve work-related emotional and family problems such as alcoholism.
- *Family Planning and Population Control.* Working with planned parenthood groups and abortion centers and providing sex-education services.
- *Private Practice.* Working with patients privately, providing psychotherapeutic services.
- *Mental Health Services.* Counseling or therapy in community mental health centers, psychiatric hospitals, and family agencies, including in- and out-patient services in psychiatric settings.

Other areas of social work endeavor include social work research, education, policy planning, and administration.

A SOCIAL WORKER IS ...

Traditionally, social workers were trained as

... *caseworkers*, who worked directly with individuals and families (further identified as psychiatric caseworkers, medical caseworkers, and family caseworkers)

... *group workers*, who worked with groups of people who had some common purpose

... *community organization workers*, who worked with community agencies and services to resolve broad community issues.

Although these approaches have many values and techniques in common, social work training, until recently, highlighted their differences. Now these designations have been eliminated by schools of social work and are no longer used in the field. In the seventies, social work training has become "generalist," designed to prepare the social worker to use any of the three approaches in any setting.

Today a social worker is

... a *counselor*, who advises, listens, provides resources.

... an *administrator*, who oversees agency functions, sets policy, allocates resources, develops programs.

... a *consultant*, who provides outside expertise, assesses programs, acts as staff teacher and administrative guide.

... a *referral agent*, who suggests other services and alternate sources of help to consumers.

... a *broker*, who intervenes between an agency and a consumer.

... a *therapist*, who provides psychotherapeutic services for individuals, families, and groups.

... an *advocate*, who represents consumers.

... an *outreach worker*, who looks for, and offers services to, people who are unaware of existing resources.

... a *social planner*, who determines and plans for the needed by a community.

... a *social activist*, who promotes and politicks for ...al change.

Within any particular field the social worker may perform a variety of functions. In any one day, for example, a community mental health worker may deal directly with the emotional problems of an individual patient *(primary therapist)*, work with the family of the patient *(family worker)*, provide information to other members of the treatment team to assist in planning *(team member)*, supervise the work of another social worker or the paraprofessional staff *(supervisor)*, help someone in the community take advantage of an agency service *(outreach worker)*, refer a consumer to services elsewhere *(referral agent)*, advise a group that is dealing with a community issue *(consultant)*, and help another agency provide more or better services to a consumer *(advocate)*.

This complex network of people-oriented services in an almost infinite number of settings complicates the attempt to sort out just what social work is. Yet there is, nevertheless, a unity underlying its varied practice settings and functions that establishes social work as a distinct profession.

PROFESSIONAL BASE OF SOCIAL WORK

Professional social work is a controlled response to human needs determined by

- a *sanction*, or permission, granted by society and/or the profession's own overseeing authorities to engage in specific activities designated as social work

- a *system of values* that protects the individual's rights to self-determination, to be treated with dignity, and to the preservation of the confidential nature of the professional exchange
- a *knowledge base* composed of the accumulating knowledge of man, including the literature of the profession itself, that further defines its activities and methods with emphasis primarily on the social sciences
- a *method base*, traditionally identified as individual casework, group work, and community organization work, more currently seen as generic skills employed as appropriate in specific situations
- a *technique base* focused on human interaction, including such skills as those involved in interviewing, assessment, intervention, and organization

SOCIAL WORK— AN EASY PROFESSION?

On the surface social work appears as a relatively simple affair consisting of little more than "doing good." And after all, how much effort does it really take to "do good"? The practice of social work, however, regardless of appearances, is one of the most challenging vocations. It is always difficult, often painful, always frustrating, and requires one to perform in ways that are different and, seemingly, impossible.

Not everyone can be a social worker. Not everyone can take the "pains" of practice—the ongoing self-examination that comes with the territory; the daily struggle to integrate new knowledge and translate it into practice, recognizing, resignedly, that today's "fact" is tomorrow's "myth"; the pain of dealing with the pain of others; and the constant sense of incompleted work because a partial resolution is what, at best, occurs. Inherent in social work is also the concept of never enough: never enough resources to cope with the problems; never enough time to do justice to the work; never enough skills or understanding to accomplish what one would like to accomplish.

Beginning social workers are often disillusioned by the recognition that there is no magic formula that once learned resolves all problems, no patent medicine to drive out the hurts of people. Theories abound, of course, but they answer only a minute percentage of the bewildering variety of complex problems confronted in daily practice.

"What should I do here?" "What should I say?" "What is the answer?" beginning students ask. The questions are frequently answered with another question: "What do you think?" Or, if a more concrete response is forthcoming, it usually indicates a direction rather than a specific formula. There are no "real answers" in the usual sense. There are areas to pursue and information to be shared; there are alternate ways of approaching problems; there are ways of rephrasing a problem to indicate a new direction to pursue; there are ways of exploring issues from fresh perspectives—but "answers" to problems are few and far between, and they are not prepackaged. They come only from a knowledge and understanding of the human condition.

Although there is a knowledge input into social work, its base is conceptual. Social work provides a framework (several, actually) through which situations and problems pass and may be better understood, recognizing that the framework remains hypothetical, based on, but not rooted in, "fact." When dealing with people who by nature are particular combinations of heredity and environment, culture and economics, logic and absurdity, sense and nonsense, the end result is not any sense of positiveness but a sense of doubt. Lacking the precision of surgical procedure, the solutions provided by social work may seem makeshift in comparison. The resolution of a problem may provide some sense of accomplishment, but rarely a "Yes, I understand *completely*!" In the process of assessing and attempting to resolve a human situation, initial questions generate more and more questions until the questions begin to contain directions toward a solution of the problem. Because of man's unpredictable nature, a social worker's responses, must, of necessity be based on probabilities.

If social work cannot provide answers, it can nevertheless provide the means to help people themselves search for their own answers. It can provide the means by which people can attain *their* own goals or even formulate new goals, but it does not provide goals.

A major pitfall facing beginning workers is the temptation to personalize situations, to impose on others, for example, their own solutions to life situations. "Look, just be like me!" "I had a problem like that and look what *I* did!" All practitioners at one time or another have muttered this to themselves. How simple it is to set oneself up as a role model for others to emulate; and how comforting to show people the "way," to tell them what to do!

In most circumstances social workers do *not* give advice. More often they provide more options and allow the consumer to choose. Social workers must respect their own values, desires, and ambitions. But consumers, too, have their own rights and needs and values, which may be similar to or different from those of the social worker. The essential task is, however, to help consumers achieve their own goals and to pursue their own destinies. The social worker often presents options, and the freedom to choose which option to those who feel they have none, and provides the means and resources through which consumers can pursue those options, but the decisions about which option to pursue and which resource to use must be made by the consumer, not by the social worker. People may be permitted to make mistakes, to fail, to take wrong turns—overall, to be responsible for their own lives. In a professional relationship with a consumer, a social worker does not ordinarily advise.

How can social workers help other people when they themselves are not sure of the answers? How can beginning social workers in their twenties, for example, be of service to a sixty-year-old foster mother, who has already reared a half dozen children of her own and also taken care of foster children for twenty years?

A social worker can help. Young students have helped experienced foster parents, male social workers have worked effectively with unwed mothers, and hopelessly in-debt social workers have helped consumers budget their money. Although social workers do not tell people what to do, they can, nevertheless, *enable* people to achieve for themselves. When this concept is grasped in depth, questions of experience, knowledge, and authority assume their proper place in the helping process; it is in the process of helping that the answer lies.

These matters, of course, mitigate against social work's being an "easy" profession. For the most part, these issues become resolved in practice, yet a sensitivity to their existence must be maintained throughout one's professional life. As ongoing conditions of social work, they require continual monitoring to keep in perspective.

In short, social work is far from easy. It requires a commitment that goes beyond intellectual demand, beyond, in many ways, the demands of other professions. As social work skills are examined in more detail, the nature of these demands will be more fully appreciated.

THE REWARDS OF SOCIAL WORK

No, it's not easy, but the rewards of social work more than

compensate for the investment. Not the least of the rewards is the deep-down sense of personal satisfaction that accompanies the work, that sense of contributing to "society." Social work identifies the practitioner directly with the forces concerned with the qualitative issues of social existence. Its purposefulness cannot be denied. The personal satisfaction derived adds another dimension to the meaningfulness of life.

An inevitable consequence of the work is that in the process of working with others social workers learn more about themselves. They are constantly called upon to examine their own motives, purposes, needs, and desires, an enriching experience in itself. As a result, social workers become more self-aware and self-understanding. One of the principles of practice, which remains constant throughout professional work, is the separation of the social worker's own life from that of the consumer. The need for *objectivity* requires this separation. To ensure that responses to others are in accordance with the needs and objectives of the consumer and not with their own, that is, to maintain the separation, social workers must constantly reexamine their own values, needs, and feelings. Working closely with people is an experience that inevitably stirs up echoes and vibrations within oneself, for basically people are not that different. But when the worker's own feelings are not successfully understood (controlled), their intrusion into the consumer/worker relationship often impedes the objectivity of the service and thus reduces the professionalism of the worker. A brief consideration of the values of self-determination and dignity, for example, strongly suggests that the use of others to answer a social worker's own problems would indeed seriously violate the code. Part of the work, then, requires constant and often revealing looks inward. Even though one's understanding of oneself is rarely articulated in direct work with consumers, such understanding nevertheless provides a base from which to work. And in gaining a new understanding of others, a worker's self-understanding, in turn, is increased, an additional reward that comes with the job.

A certain exhilaration is derived from working with people simply because people are interesting. Often unpredictable, sometimes bizarre (in terms of one's own orientation), and always challenging, people are exciting to work with. The development of an understanding of people (and of themselves) and of some of the factors that influence life situations is an ongoing process that is indigenous to the work. It is an effort that is constantly revealing, although a total understanding of human beings—interacting with themselves, with others, with their total environment—can never be achieved because each individual understanding produces, in turn, new questions and new directions to pursue. Social workers are nevertheless privileged to get glimmerings of the human condition, however awesome in its complexity, and that, in itself, is a reward.

It is tempting to say that professional satisfactions are enjoyed when people's lives are better as a consequence of one's involvement, but it would not be entirely accurate. Although social workers provide the access by which people derive more satisfactions from their lives, the decision making, the actions, and the responsibilities lie with those who can avail themselves of the service. It is *their* responsibility if their lives improve and *their* responsibility if they do not. Responsibility cannot be only for success. If social workers were to take credit for consumers' accomplishments, they must also assume the responsibility for their defeats. To burden social workers with the responsibility for the suicide, the divorce, the delinquency, and the emotional problems of people is a bit much. In fairness then, the satisfaction comes from the *doing* of the work, from the use of oneself as a professional instrument.

"Helping people to help themselves" can be understood in this context. The task of social work is to help people to assume as much command over their own lives as possible; to help people to assume positions of responsibility in order to enhance their own existence. When consumers "succeed," it is the result of their own strengths and abilities, assisted by the social worker who helps the consumer to "exploit" these strengths. On the other hand, when a person fails, it is because insufficient strength was available. Social workers provide the "means" toward accomplishment. If there are barriers in the way of accomplishment, social workers remove or level those barriers insofar as possible. Social workers must examine their skills critically; perhaps an old skill needs modification or a new skill needs to be developed. Workers must continue to recognize that there is no magic and that there are limitations to understanding at any given time.

The responsibilities inherent in the task of helping others professionally are enormous. But realistically, social workers can do what they can do in accordance with the existing realities. Social workers create neither slums nor ghettos nor unemployment, nor mental and physical handicaps, nor unemployment, nor illness, nor injustice, nor juvenile delinquency, nor child abuse, nor any of the countless other social dysfunctionings to which people are subject. They try, of course, to alleviate these conditions and to mitigate their effects on human beings, but in the here and now such conditions must be accepted as being real and potent. The effects of grinding poverty on an infant will *never* be totally eliminated—mitigated, perhaps, but not eliminated. Social workers can help people achieve their maximum potential; that is their task. At the same time, however, it would be patently absurd to believe that several hours or even days with a social worker would undo a lifetime of conditioning. More tangible results may be noted in the execution of the tasks of daily living where the service is designed to meet specific aspects of day-to-day survival—delivering specific services, providing information, job referrals, budget balancing, and so on. But here, of course, the consumer already has the strengths to cope with community living at least on a minimal level.

By combining one's knowledge with one's assumptions and experience, under a mantle of professional self-discipline and established skills resting on a base of professional values, the "art" of social work practice is revealed. And therein lies the excitement of social work as a profession.

Although basic knowledge outlines the grand contours of social work practice, the actual specifics of practice are less charted and rely more on individual skills and applications rather than professional fiat. Specific work situations indicate general principles of practice that are applicable, but in each individual situation there is also a certain uniqueness that must be addressed.

But after many years in the field, a social worker may say, "The same old problems over and over again and I am offering the same old solutions." At times the sheer enormity of the daily task and the massive volume of work can literally force the practitioner into a severely routinized practice.

From the beginning social worker's point of view, however, the uniqueness of each particular case may be literally overwhelming. In dealing with case after case, each one "unique," the new practitioner may be overpowered by a sense of impotency. How can one possibly work with so many different situations? Are there no generalized rules?

Balance is the key to social work practice—balancing the commonality of human experiences with the uniqueness of the individual experience, balancing the social environment with individual needs, balancing the real world with the fantasy world, balancing Darwinism with humanism, balancing hopes with realities, surpluses with scarcities. It is in the process of balancing that the true excitement of social work occurs.

A FACT OF LIFE—
POWER IN SOCIAL WORK

Intervention by the social worker in the life of another person introduces the concept of power; even though the interventions are based on the best of intentions, power is nevertheless a recognizable factor in the relationship. Power, the ability to control and to influence others, is a recognized factor in all people-to-people relationships; its significance in professional relationships is considerable. Power in and of itself is neither good nor bad; it is simply there. It can be used either constructively or destructively. To begin to understand power in social work relationships, a consideration of the consumers who use the services of the social worker is in order. Consumers are divided into two categories, *voluntary* and *nonvoluntary*, with various stages in between.

Voluntary consumers recognize the need for some sort of service and seek assistance from social workers on their own. Implicit in the voluntary approach is an acknowledgment that the social worker has something to offer—just what that something is may be vague, but the social worker is recognized as a "helping" source. As long as the social worker is seen, realistically or not, as being in a position to provide that help, the worker is in a position of power. More often than not, the power ascribed to the social worker is more fiction than fact. The need to receive help, however, tends to bias the consumer's perception of reality. Physical illness often ascribes a similar power to the physician, and many medical "cures" are based on this distortion.

Social workers often experience a sense of gratification in being seen in a position of magnified power, for all too often they feel a sense of powerlessness in confronting the multitude of problems with which they are forced to deal, problems that often defy resolution. Being perceived as a "super power" by a consumer thus offers a much needed ego stroke, which is especially welcomed by beginning workers. The great expectations placed on beginning workers by consumers are sometimes quite frightening, and the worker may react with a frenzied round of activity or a paralyzing fear that inhibits all activity, literally denying the authority that the worker actually has. In an attempt to enhance the good feeling of being needed and being powerful generated by the consumer's false perception of the power of the worker, the new worker may overtly or perhaps very subtly encourage this artificial image. When this occurs, the consumer is serving the worker's needs, rather than the worker serving the consumer's needs—a reversal of roles.

Nonvoluntary consumers—the prisoner, the parolee, the probationer, the child abuser, the abused child, the foster child, the "negligent" parent, the child with behavioral problems, the truant—are referred to social workers by various institutions of society. Because such consumers have not elected the service on their own volition, they tend to view the social worker somewhat differently. Here the worker often represents social authority, the larger controlling forces that seek to modify existing behavioral patterns or even the circumstances of living itself. The anger felt by nonvoluntary consumers against society is consequently often directed toward the worker.

Thus the role of authority in a professional interaction has an impact on both the consumer, voluntary and nonvoluntary, and the worker. How such authority is handled depends on the worker's recognition of the power roles of the respective parties, the contract between the worker and the consumer, and the resources of the agency. A mutually trusting relationship can best be developed by the recognition of the reality of the situation and a clarification of the real and imagined powers between the parties. Failure to recognize the role of power in a professional interaction allows its uncontrolled influence to aggravate the difficulties in, and sometimes even destroy, the interaction.

SOCIAL WORK— ROOTS AND BRANCHES

Although the philosophical roots of social work are deeply embedded in England from the point of view of value and model, social work came to be an organized discipline in the United States as a direct result of the Industrial Revolution.

The Industrial Revolution radicalized not only the means of production but also the processes through which man lives with man. During the rapid technological explosion of the 1800s, centuries of established values, which had served preindustrialized America well, were overturned. Mass migrations and monumental shifts in population across the country and the clustering of people in new patterns of living brought an end to traditional ways of coping with man's relationship to man.

The Industrial Revolution urbanized the United States, as people clustered in increasing numbers around the newly expanding means of production, the factories. Immigrants poured into the United States from Europe, bringing with them new languages, new ethics, new familial and personal value systems. American families themselves began to relocate, huddling in the expanding cities. Nineteenth-century United States presented a contradictory picture of both order and disorder, order in the rational arrangements of mechanized industry, the mechanization of time, and the mechanization of the order of work, disorder of the human variety produced by the massive social upheavals provoked by the new machine.

The traditional role of the family was shattered. In the small-town and village life of the preindustrial era, the family and the extended family were all important units. Many of the problems of people interacting with one another could be most effectively handled on the family level. Problems of health, finances, education, marriage, and such were situations best handled within the family unit. It was only in matters of protection or in trade between families or villages that other systems came into play. The family unit was the key to survival.

The Industrial Revolution severely eroded the survival base of the family system. It brought workers to factories, to the centers of production. People left villages to gather in anonymous cities; living became crowded and vertical. The immigrants and native Americans from different sections of the country brought to the cities their different values and attitudes, which were reflected in the problems that this new "rubbing shoulders" began to produce. As a unit, the family could no longer deal with these new social complexities; the sheer enormity and range of the problems defied the family's ability to cope. Juvenile delinquency, no longer an aberration of an individual family member, assumed increased social consequence with the development of gangs that systematically patrolled the streets and terrorized tenement dwellers. The very proximity of families living together introduced health problems that afflicted not only family members but whole buildings and blocks and neighborhoods as well. Even the education of their children could no longer be responsibly assumed by parents. The world was blossoming with opportunities and possibilities—and difficulties. Urban survival could not be left to the limited interests and knowledge of the individual family.

The immigrant waves and the uprooting of masses of Americans transformed a horizontal agricultural landscape to a vertical city-scape of tall buildings and tenements. The physical change was accompanied by value changes. The traditional roles of family and church as propagators of values and belief systems were radically altered by the new agglomeration of people and the new and bewildering demands that mechanized production made on people's lives and values. Along with turmoil, the Industrial Revolution produced a new class, the middle class, and a new youth phenomenon, "adolescence." In the search for social order obliterated in the new chaos lay the seeds of social work.

Prior to the nineteenth century the predominant philosophy of Calvinism carried with it the belief in the inevitability of life as it is. Thus, misery and need were also inevitable conditions of man. Life was a closed system within which man must accept his chosen lot; there was little to be done about the forces that control man's destiny. Poverty was seen as part and parcel of the natural order of things, and an individual's right to help and assistance was built into the laws of the time. The community's response to need was traditionally generous (not by today's standards but significant in the society of scarcity that existed). To counter Calvinism's inevitable fatalism, the Industrial Revolution in the nineteenth century carried with it a utopian concept of infinite progress. Through industry and mechanization, life could be altered. Visions of equality and abundance drifted temptingly on the horizon. Man began to sense that he could "conquer" life through work; through work came opportunity. Along with this optimism came a much more suspicious view of poverty and dependency. Because poverty was no longer considered an inevitable consequence of life, a failure to rise above poverty must somehow be the responsibility of the individual suffering from it. The concept of "need" as part of the natural order of things gave way to another doctrine: that a *moral flaw* in the individual was responsible for economic dependence. Although not a new concept, the moral flaw doctrine assumed increased significance during the Industrial Revolution and represented an important shift in values, a revitalization of the "work ethic," the physical labor of individuals being a necessary condition for survival. (Interpretation of the work ethic has become increasingly sophisticated. Poverty, for example, is no longer considered a "moral flaw" within the individual; now it is thought by many to be a "psychological aberration" that requires corrective intervention.)

Industrialization and urbanization, a laissez-faire philosophy that emphasized individual responsibility, the Darwinian postulate of "survival of the fittest"—what then of the poor, how were they to be viewed? As the unfit, weak, flawed, unworthy— objects of contempt.

The laboring classes, the working poor, those destined to keep the factories humming (and the profits and the power accumulating), were kept as close to a level of dependency as possible without actually becoming dependent. The working poor became the most conspicuously applauded members of the new social order. Work, in and of itself, had assumed a virtue close to religion. Material accumulations now became the ultimate purpose of life, the highest good man could attain. Although labor itself rarely led to an accumulation of wealth for the worker, its glorification led to the growing wealth of others.

The early social workers were concerned with delinquency, family breakup, sanitation and health problems, the economic fragility of existence, and the disruption of traditional value systems. They themselves were drawn from the upper-middle and upper classes. Motivated by altruistic and humanistic feelings, they were nevertheless untrained and unskilled. By contemporary standards their work would be considered inept, biased by their own concepts of right and wrong, hopelessly judgmental. The early social worker, the "friendly visitor," attempted to mediate the gross social inequities of the day. The essential work of the friendly visitors was to provide *concrete* services. They supplied food and clothing, paid the rent, summoned the doctor. The price for the services was often a sermon or a statement of moral philosophy.

As social problems proliferated, the energies of the charity workers, the friendly visitors, were simply not sufficient to meet the needs of the poor, neither in quality nor in quantity. The need for trained service agents rather than untrained volunteers was slowly recognized. During World War I social work began to emerge as a professional discipline.

The social problems brought to light by the Great Depression in 1929 produced an expansion in the field of social work. Schools of social work, under university auspices, began to offer professional training in the field during the twenties and thirties. Standards and criteria for professional practice were identified and promoted. Social work skills were identified and became integral components in the training process. As training in any field requires identification of boundaries and limits, social work training led to a categorization of skills, to specialization.

The broad field of social problems became area identified and social workers were trained to work in specific service areas: family social worker, child social worker, medical social worker, psychiatric social worker. Gone was the *generalist* function of the friendly visitor who had responded to whatever problem required attention. Area specialists functioned out of their specific expertise. An obvious parallel exists in medicine, where the general practitioner has almost disappeared in favor of the medical specialist. Having a more expert knowledge in a more narrowly focused area, the social worker specialist attacked social problems through problem isolation and detailed study within the isolation.

The new professionals soon recognized that social problems were more than manifestations of individual malaise. Social problems were, rather, manifestations of the social, economic, and political system. The question became whether to work to correct the system or to work with the victims of the system. The professional field opted to work with the victims primarily, and both the quality and the content of professional social work training were influenced by this decision.

The decision was a difficult one and, as mentioned earlier, arguments can be presented on either side. It must be recognized, however, that social work is mandated by the society and is primarily funded by society. Unlike other professions—medical and legal, for example—where payment is made directly by the consumer, social work depends principally on public financing. To a large extent, therefore, the profession of social work must reflect the prevailing values, assumptions, and attitudes of the social system. As a consequence, the practice of social work is basically concerned with helping the victim rather than alleviating the causes of the problem.

Although the industrialized countries of western Europe had early on instituted public-welfare services, the United States lagged considerably behind until the passage of the Social Security Act in 1935, which served to move social service from the private sector to the public sector; it was a dawning recognition by the government that a public apparatus must be made available to meet the social needs of its citizenry.

In the 1930s the works of Sigmund Freud influenced the development of social work in the United States. Freud offered not only an understanding of the human psyche but also a method of treatment that could help man to cope more productively with his life. Its subsequent modifications as a treatment instrument provided both a therapeutic tool for the nonmedical person and a solution to a problem that had been plaguing social workers. The rise of the public agency had eroded the prime purpose of the private and voluntary agencies, which was the provision of concrete services. Psychotherapeutic techniques offered a new service, *mental health* to the needy. The nonpublic agencies could thus justify their continued survival. As social work moved eagerly toward the fields of psychiatry and psychology, the distinction between social work and the other professional mental-health disciplines became blurred.

Generally, social workers were not sufficiently trained for the practice of psychotherapy, which is a specialist function. The two-year graduate program did not really provide sufficient expertise for true professional practice. Within the broad panorama of social work's interests, the graduate program in psychotherapy could offer only the beginnings of theory and limited experience in practice. More important, however, psychotherapy could not be a *prime* instrument for helping the poor. Successful psychotherapy demands upon a set of preconditions: an ability to abstract to a degree, an awareness of one's feelings, and a sense of something within oneself that one wishes to change. For various reasons, many of the poor do not fit into that attitudinal or value system.

One of the many results of this professional stance was to alienate some of the poor and to dissuade them from seeking out social work as a helping force. Another result was the movement of social work from the poor, whom it was designed to serve, to the middle and upper classes who could benefit from these particular services.

Social work has subsequently evolved a mixture of practice techniques that combines psychodynamic understanding with environmental intervention. The movement today is away from the narrow specialist role of the social worker toward a broader, more *generalist* function. In short, the social worker is being trained to offer more than one service option to the potential consumer. Professional service is based more on the needs of consumers in *their* situations than on the specialized skills of the social worker.

Most recent developments in the field place social work practice more specifically within a social environmental context. The concept of an *ecosystem*, the human organism and its adaptive fit in its total environment, has been established as the conceptual base from which future practice will flow.

TWO

SOCIAL WORK VALUES—PERMANENT AND CHANGING

PERMANENT VALUES

Because social work is relatively unencumbered by objective performance criteria, and because those standards that are available are not particularly efficient in judging performance effectiveness, the value base of social work itself serves as the principal standard by which effectiveness is measured. The value base of social work—self-determination, the dignity of the individual, and the confidentiality of communication—has remained essentially unchanged since its inception, despite changes in terminology. Various practice techniques evolve from time to time and one methodology gives way to another, but the value base—the trademark of social work practice—remains firm.

The integrity of the work is determined by adherence to the value base; an evaluation of the work is thus made by judging the practice against the standards. The measurement of performance—the consideration of the practice situation in relation to the value system—is most helpful for the experienced professional as well as the beginner. For example, despite an obvious need for medical services that can be provided only in a nursing home, sick consumer, Ms. Norris, seventy-seven, prefers to remain in her own three-story walk-up tenement, where she has lived for the past fifteen years. To consider this situation in terms of the value base of social work, the following situation must be considered. While shopping, Ms. Norris fell and fractured her hip. Hospitalized for six weeks, she is now ready for discharge. In addition to her hip injury and her advanced age, Ms. Norris has other physical ailments. At this point she is unable to bear any weight on her hip, nor is she able to use a crutch or a walker because of both the hip injury and a real fear of falling again. For a period of time, Ms. Norris will be confined to a wheelchair.

Ms. Norris has no family. Neither are friends available to help as Ms. Norris is essentially a loner. A nursing home is recommended for a period of time. The next best alternative, a visiting nurse service, would be available for only a limited period each day and would not provide the minimum medical care Ms. Norris needs now in her rehabilitation program. After studying the total situation, the social worker recognizes that nursing home care would provide the safest and quickest way for Ms. Norris to return to the community and her accustomed life-style. But, on broaching the possibility of a short-term stay in a nursing home, Ms. Norris will hear none of it. She will not rationally discuss any alternative but an immediate return to her home.

These are the value questions the social worker must consider: Does the consumer have the right to choose and to live by her choices? Does she have the right to make "erroneous" choices? How much social work "intervention" is required here? Are the concepts of dignity being overridden by presumed knowledge of what is best? Is our understanding of "most appropriate" or "in the best interests of" overriding the principle of self-determination? If so, should it? Are there times when social control is more important than self-generated decision making? Is this one of those times?

The three basic values that seem to resist the tides of growth and change that periodically inundate the field are *self-determi-*

nation, the *dignity of the individual*, and the *confidentiality of communication*.

Without adherence to such values, social work ceases to be a professional service and becomes exploitative. Without these values as true guides, social work is easily distorted, for the power inherent in the role of the helping person becomes subverted to one of domination and control, and the practice itself becomes so vague and directionless as to be self-serving and meaningless.

Self-determination

Self-determination is the fundamental right of people to make their own choices in life; to decide on and direct the course of their own lives. One important task of the social worker is to help people choose the course most appropriate for them by providing information about the variety of options and the access routes to various options and by removing the obstacles, internal or external, standing in the way of choice making. Although self-determination in practice is not easily achieved, it nevertheless remains a primary goal of social work.

People are often unable to exercise self-determination because they *feel* incapable of making choices. In such situations the social worker explores with the consumer those feelings—feelings of inadequacy, overreaction to risk taking or mistake making, fears of loss of control—that are blocking the exercise of choice. A person may not know that choice exists: that there is legal protection against rent gouging, for example, or that a neighborhood service provides free camp experiences for children, or that one has the right to protest a decision made by the Department of Social Services. Here, of course, social workers inform consumers about these alternatives to various situations and answer questions that will enable consumers to arrive at decisions reflecting their own best interests. Perhaps there are few or no choices available. A mother, for example, may need a nursery program for her preschooler in order to free her to seek employment or to return to school herself. If no nursery programs are available, the social worker may help develop this service for the community. In the meantime, this mother might use a nursery program in another community or financial assistance might be provided to hire a baby-sitter, or the worker might form a group of other mothers (or fathers) with similar problems who can share baby-sitting responsibilities. In this way the social worker has provided greater choice options for mothers in this situation.

In self-determination, insofar as possible, the choice must remain with the consumer. Such choices may be made against the worker's considered judgment or knowledge, but it must be understood that the consumer has the right to make mistakes, to commit errors, to not take advantage of his entitlements, to remain dependent rather than become independent, poor rather than rich, dishonest rather than honest, to be on public assistance rather than to take a job, and so on. The consumer has the right to make a whole series of choices that social workers would not consider the best. The consequences of choices rest, of course, with the person making those choices. The consumer has the right to make all sorts of ''good'' and ''bad'' choices, including the right to refuse the social worker's helpful assistance.

The concept of the consumer's right to reject the social worker's assistance is often difficult for the beginning social worker to accept. How can anyone turn away assistance when it is pleasantly offered, when there are no strings attached, when it is obviously for the person's own good?

The person's own ''good'' must be defined individually not socially. Within the limits of competency and noninfringement on the rights of others, one may pursue one's own life course. People have the right to determine their own cadence, their own direction, to march to their own drumbeats. The task of the social worker is to enter, *with permission*, the world of the other person, to help remove the barriers blocking the pursuit of their visions or to help alter those visions to make them more attainable. Insofar as is appropriately possible, this is accomplished within the framework of the consumer's life; the ultimate decision as to which direction to take and perhaps even the fact of life itself must remain in the control of the consumer.

The principle of self-determination protects the consumer from the certainty of the social worker. The myth that the social worker (by virtue of the understanding, ability to listen, empathy, and support conveyed) has a special knowledge of life and can be relied upon to make the decisions for the consumer is just that, of course, a myth, although some workers are nevertheless tempted. Faced with the many human problems that come through the door, with their agonizing frustrations and the often seen *angst* of the human condition, social workers ache to cut through the complex process of helping people to make their *own* decisions and to offer, instead, their own solutions to consumers' problems. How much easier it seems to solve problems for people rather than to have people solve problems for themselves. When the social worker usurps the rights and prerogatives of choice, the consumer is robbed of the personal value inherent in the decision-making process. Neither the wisdom nor the correctness of perception, nor the rightness of such decisions represents sufficient justification for such intervention. The process of life depends not on ''being'' there but on ''getting'' there. By denying the consumer the experience of ''getting'' there, the social worker denies a most significant element of life, the responsibility for one's own destiny.

The concept of self-determination, thus far, seems relatively simple: The social worker's job is merely to help people to help themselves. But social workers work with not only healthy normal adults but all people. The more the concept of self-determination is pursued, the more its seemingly black-and-white issues become various shades of gray. In negotiating this grayish landscape, the social worker becomes aware that the principle of self-determination cannot be exercised universally. Self-determination may be denied, for example, to psychotics, psychiatrically defined as having "lost touch with reality." Society allows psychotics to be, at times, institutionalized against their will, medicated or treated without informed consent, and so on. Freedom to participate in self-determination is denied psychotics to protect them from harming themselves or others. This denial of self-determination has been the subject of increasing controversy. Advocates demanding a redefinition of psychosis and an increased recognition of the civil and legal rights of the mentally ill have appeared. Newspaper horror stories of people institutionalized for years for deviancy have created support for the movement, which carries sufficient weight to at least question the amount of control that society can exercise over its so-called mentally disturbed. How much self-determination can society rightfully deny? Does society have the right to protect itself? If so, how much protection is necessary? How much control should be exercised against those so identified? Although no one is arguing against humane treatment for the mentally ill, the issue of "forcing" humane treatment on the mentally ill is debatable.

The principles of self-determination can be violated when a "super issue," an issue of life or death, is involved. Surely persons should be stopped from jumping off buildings when under the delusion that they can fly. The irreversible consequences of this act deny self-determination by reasons of insanity. Would it follow, however, that *all* cases of threatened suicide should be denied self-determination? The answer may be an unqualified "yes" in many cases, where it would be permitted by the psychiatric designation of temporary insanity; in other cases, however, it may be a very doubtful "yes" or even a "no." Should terminally ill patients who are in great pain be allowed to select their death? Should suicide be denied to those hopeless, dehumanized people confined in concentration camps? An automobile accident has turned an athletic thirty-year-old man into a quadriplegiac. In pain, unable to care for simple bodily functions, unable to continue his active life-style, unwilling to radically adjust to an intellectual life-style that is practically all that is left to him, the young man pleads for the means to end his own life. What is the answer? Easy yes and no answers are, of course, elusive.

Granted that self-determination should be denied in certain cases, the question remains, at what point along the mental health continuum do the rights of self-determination become void? Do psychotics have any rights of self-determination? Can a person, for example, opt for insanity over sanity in this world? In a recent experimental treatment for schizophrenia a dialysis procedure, which literally washs the blood of the patient, was used. Early results of the procedure are encouraging. Patients who had spent years in institutions returned to the community to lead apparently normal lives, free from psychotic episodes. The treatment required patients to undergo an eight-hour dialysis procedure once a month for the rest of their lives; eight hours each month in return for sanity. A number of patients refused the treatment. They preferred sickness to health, insanity to sanity. Some patients rejected the "cure" because of the amount of time spent in the dialysis procedure; others felt that sanity would rob them of something that was exclusively their own, their creativity, their uniqueness, their dreams. Do these people have the right to decide to remain insane, and consequently institutionalized, rather than to become sane and participate in the community? One position argues that being insane precludes any decision making regarding sanity. The other position advocates that, sane or insane, people have the right to choose.

The "shopping-bag lady" has become a frequent sight on the inner-city landscape. A woman of almost any age, she may be seen bearing numerous stuffed shopping bags, often heavily weighted. When not parked in one spot surrounded by her bags, she can be seen laboriously wending her way down a street. Often the very number of bags impedes her travels. Since she cannot carry them all at once, she takes a few, advances a few steps, puts them down, retraces her steps for the remaining shopping bags, over and over again until her journey's end. Her bags contain nothing more than accumulated deposits from trash baskets, empty bottles, old newspapers, and cardboard cartons. Her body is often heavily bound in rags and old clothes, and her face is usually protected from the world by mufflers or masks or sunglasses. Frequently the shopping-bag lady sleeps on the street, huddled in doorways or near cellars for protection against the weather. Her contact with others is minimal, just enough to survive.

Many services are available to the shopping-bag lady. Adequate shelter can be provided, hot meals, clothing, medical attention, a range of social services. But the shopping-bag lady will have none of them, no matter how deferentially they are offered. Attempts to reach her have been futile. The shopping-bag lady remains, however, a pitiable individual, seemingly in need of help. The question of self-determination remains. Do shopping-bag ladies have the right to refuse the offers of help that have been forthcoming? Do they have the right to refuse a decent place to live? To refuse wholesome food? Good medical attention? Do they have the right to maintain their own life-style even though it endangers their lives? Or, must someone else make those decisions for them?

Is self-determination only for the normal, healthy person, and if so, who defines "normal" and "healthy"? Is society unable to tolerate any deviance? Must all decision making and all human activities be defined in terms of the statistical norm? Aware of the probability that the art might change and not necessarily for the better, would one forcibly treat a mad van Gogh? Particularly in working with the emotionally disturbed, these are the questions the social worker must respond to on almost a daily basis. How are responses determined?

First, it is most important to recognize the value issue underlying the practical issue of the problem itself. When a patient, for example, refuses psychotropic medication, the practical issue is what should be done. The value issue goes to a deeper level. What are the limits of the social worker's activity in helping the person to take the medication? An attempt to understand the patient's resistance to the medication is in order, followed by efforts to overcome the resistance—explaining how the medication works, discussing the side effects, informing the patient about dosage, and so on. Here the social worker is well within the bounds of professional values. When this approach proves futile and the patient remains adamant in refusing to take the medication, is the social worker then permitted to deliberately bias the information, to distort the facts to make the medication more attractive, downgrading, for example, the side effects, accentuating the benefits. The ends again are good; the means are questionable. Does mental illness necessarily sanction the social worker's "gentle" efforts to limit self-determination? Can consumers be placed in positions where they virtually have no choice but to take the medication?

These issues require more than the decision of a single social worker with a single consumer. These questions should be directed to the social agency that sanctions the work of the social worker. By conferring with the supervisor and other agency executives, the social worker can formulate a workable policy for the consumer. Obviously, social workers themselves can make significant contributions to the decision making and should so express themselves in this council. Mitigating factors may occur in any individual case that would favor various solutions; thus whatever conclusion an agency comes to regarding any particular situation may have to be reconsidered in another.

The interpretation or revocation of self-determination is also subject to debate in the field of child care, where workers are confronted daily with such questions. The principle of self-determination is significant in work with children. It is sufficient here to recognize that for children as a group, self-determination is a limited concept.

Prisoners, at first glance, appear to have their rights of self-determination severely restricted. Actually, however, only their physical freedom has been denied. They are making decisions all the time—whether to obey or to break the rules, to go to the machine shop or to the laundry, to be nice to a fellow prisoner or to cut him, to survive or not, not unlike the choices open to all.

In the prison setting, or in a similar confining situation, the social worker can help the inmates to discover the limits of their options and to make choices within those limits. There are almost always choices available, no matter how insignificant they may at first appear to be. It is in the exercise of choice, of self-determination, that the true sense of self-respect is found.

The concept of self-determination permeates all social work practice. Can one, for example, start a community program without the informed consent of the community? Can one help a person to change a situation if that person has not determined that the situation should be changed? Social workers must be constantly aware that, despite their good intentions, their considerable knowledge and expertise, and all their years of professional experience, the consumer always has the right to refuse the service. Although social workers may present their services in a most positive manner and attempt to work on the person's "resistance" to service, the consumer always has the ultimate right to say "no."

Then there are those consumers who want *all* service, who want the social worker to make their decisions, to tell them what to do, to exercise their rights of self-determination. The temptation to respond positively to this situation is sometimes overwhelming.

The truly skilled professional social worker is able to offer consumers the knowledge, the understanding, and/or the means by which they can make their own decisions to live their own lives in the manner and style they see as appropriate. Only in those situations where consumers are unable to participate in, or are prohibited from, making choices can the social worker assume the role of decision maker. When the social worker must intervene, either by law or by professional obligation, such intervention should be minimal, the fundamental task being to restore the right of self-determination as quickly as possible.

The Dignity of the Individual

In the course of a workday, a social worker deals with a wide variety of people who differ in countless ways, including ethnic and religious backgrounds as well as degrees of mental health. Although some consumers may fall within the worker's own cultural or ethnic experience, others often represent cultures and values different from, or even antithetical to, the worker's. As human beings, social workers have their own share of prejudices, their own sense of right and wrong, and even their own hang-ups about groups and types of people. Like everyone else, social workers are entitled to these feelings—but not while on the job.

When the social worker is working with a consumer, that consumer is entitled to respect, dignity, and consideration regardless of skin color, age, ethnicity, national origin, and so on—*without qualification*. Once again, in the business of social work a principle simply stated can be arduous in practice. For example, the consumer is a mother who abuses her child—the bruises, the child's pain are obvious. How does the worker respond to this mother? Outrage? Horror? Condemnation? Does the worker turn from this mother with repugnance? The value of dignity requires that this mother be treated with as much respect as any other consumer. In a professional situation the dignity of the person takes precedence over the activity of the person regardless of the outrage committed, to whom it was addressed, including the social worker. The principle of dignity neither condones nor condemns the consumer's activity; it acknowledges the person.

Social workers cannot permit personal feelings, emotions, and attitudes to determine their activities. All people in trouble, all people seeking help must be treated with equal dignity and respect; they must be recognized as human beings who are attempting to deal with the world in the best way they know how—*regardless of how the worker may feel about them*. The consumer's essential worthiness as a person deserves recognition despite any other factor. A consumer who is dirty, odoriferous, or who has just urinated in his trousers is entitled to the same respect that would be accorded a pin-striped, vested, cravated executive from IBM who is having marital problems.

The profession of social work is selected by people who have more than a fair share of humanistic leanings and are less apt to be consumed by prejudice. "Less" is the key word. Although sainthood is not expected, it would be naive to assume that prejudice escapes social workers totally. The social worker's prejudices, however, must be confined to off-duty hours. In the work situation, no prejudices may be permitted to intrude. Social workers are not permitted to act on their personal feelings, likes and dislikes in their contact with consumers. All consumers are treated with equal dignity.

All social workers cannot deal with all situations, however. When personal feelings interfere sufficiently to prevent workers from performing objectively with respect to consumers they should, of course, withdraw. Many social workers cannot work with a mother who abuses her child, for example, because their personal feelings overwhelm attempts at objectivity and the value considerations of the work. The professional social worker's self-understanding allows the recognition of this occurrence. Occasionally this conflict can be resolved through supervision; if not, it is better for all concerned that the case be reassigned. Such obvious conflicts can be avoided from the outset if social workers seek employment in only those agencies that deal with the kinds of cases they prefer. Jewish social workers, for example, would most often avoid working with Nazi-oriented persons, black social workers with southern rednecks.

During social work training considerable effort is made to help students to recognize and deal with their own feelings and prejudices. The worker must be able to recognize them, compartmentalize them, and then proceed with the work at hand. In many situations the process requires a simple recognition on the worker's part.

The social worker may experience strong feelings about a consumer not because of any long-standing prejudice or personal bias but because of a current personal involvement that the social worker himself is experiencing. The consumer may present a problem that the worker is coping with in his own life, or the consumer may remind the worker of somebody with whom he is quite angry at the moment—all of which may temporarily bias the worker in his objective and dignified dealings with the consumer. Recognized as a short-term episode, the social worker may deal with the problem himself or seek help through the supervisory process.

The social work candidate who feels incapable of coping with a number of various personality types in an objective and dignified manner or who feels there are too many situations that might cause similar reactions might do well to pause here to consider whether social work is really the most appropriate career to pursue. Basically, social work requires a genuine concern for people. A genuine concern cannot be taught. What can be taught is a deeper understanding of one's own personal feelings and the methods by which they can be controlled to provide more effective service.

All people deserve dignity and respect. In some situations the social worker may be the only person who can provide it. It is easy to point a finger and cry "shame"; it is easy to express outrage and scornfully condemn activity and behavior. To recognize the human being beneath the act and to accord that human being the dignity he or she deserves is the essential first step in reaching that person in order to help them. From a recognition of the essential worthwhileness of *people*, help can be given regardless of who or what the consumer is, regardless of his or her assets and liabilities, regardless of the act he or she may or may not have committed. Recognition of human dignity is the basic first move in social work practice.

Confidentiality of Communication

The nature of the work requires consumers to share with social workers a quantity of information about themselves—the facts and circumstances of their lives, their feelings, innermost thoughts, information about their families and their friends, the state of their health, finances, beliefs, sex lives, dreams and aspirations. The communication between a social worker and a consumer often covers the entire spectrum of information, thoughts, and feelings. The nature of the communication is defined by the problem facing the consumer and by the nature of the agreement as to what work is to transpire. The huge amount of both verbal and documentary material that is divulged in a consumer/worker relationship must remain confidential unless mutually agreed to be otherwise. Confidential means, of course, that the communication is private. Confidentiality, however, extends beyond the communication itself to the fact that the consumer's presence in the relationship is often considered confidential as well.

The confidential nature of the professional relationship cannot be overstressed. The information shared by the consumer cannot even be communicated to different social service agencies without the informed consent of the consumer. When a person chooses to transfer from one agency to another in search of service, whether or not the new agency is to know about the current relationship is the consumer's decision.

Once again, although the concept of confidentiality is relatively simple to grasp, in actual practice both its gray areas and its practical limits will prove troublesome.

Social workers who are employees of an agency system, representing and being sanctioned by the agency, are obliged to report and to document their activities to the agency. Files or case records are kept on all contacts and activities of the social worker in order to validate the worker's activity, maintain quality control, assess agency effectiveness, and as a resource for future activity on the case.

Access to these records is determined by agency policy. Records are most often typed by secretaries, thus making the material available to any number of nonprofessional staff. Supervisors and agency administrators must also have access to the records. Each agency maintains its own "security" system in regard to its files. In actual practice then, the principle of confidentiality extends beyond the social worker/consumer relationship. This simple fact of social work procedure must be properly communicated to consumers so that they may know exactly what is meant by the term "confidential" at the outset of the relationship. All too often the "confidential" nature of the transaction is implied rather than detailed. Being assured by the social worker that their work together is "confidential," the consumer *assumes* that the confidentiality is between the social worker and himself, not between a service system and himself. The prospective consumer should know the limits of the confidentiality.

Confidentiality means that the consumer's right to privacy must be respected insofar as possible. It means that the social worker does *not* discuss consumers or their affairs outside the legitimate confines of the agency. If a situation is to be discussed outside the agency as learning tool, for example, the material should be disguised to prevent recognition of the people involved. Consumers, of course, can give informed consent to have information about themselves made available to others outside the service delivery system. Seemingly innocuous comments about a person that in the normal course of things would be mentioned without thinking become articles of consideration in professional interchanges. What information should be shared with the service delivery system and whether it should be confined within that service delivery system is a decision to be made by the consumer. Even mention by one system to another that a person is a consumer is a violation of confidentiality, as is the taping and observation of consumers without their consent.

The limits to confidentiality, like the limits to other social work values, are difficult to designate. When working with the mentally ill, the senile, or with children, the limits of self-determination reemerge. How much of the decision making regarding privacy can be realistically left to these particular consumers? The response to this question is determined by the significance of the material and its potential use; the principle regarding confidentiality, however, is like that of self-determination—the rights to privacy must be respected as much as realistically possible.

In some situations people lose the right to privacy, prisoners, for example, and mental patients involuntarily committed. For the most part, however, confidentiality can be breached only when the potential consequences resulting from the disclosure are deemed to be more significant than the maintenance of the value. For example, a consumer might discuss a homicide he is planning to commit, or he may reveal an intention to commit suicide. If the social worker were to suspect execution of the thought in action, would confidentiality remain intact? Do the ''super'' issues of life or death override the concept of confidentiality? It would appear so.

In the case of contemplated suicide, the social worker, after conferring with the supervisor, may decide to violate confidentiality by calling the police or getting in touch with the consumer's relatives. It is often assumed that the consumer is communicating this information because there is a part of him that wants to be stopped. Although this assumption may be valid, it may also allow the worker a ''rationalization'' for the violation of confidentiality, particularly if it is felt that a rationalization is needed.

In dealing with a suicidal consumer, the social worker should initially attempt to ''work it out,'' that is, assess the consequences of the action, determine the cause, and help the consumer deal with his feelings in a less self-destructive manner. Only when all else has failed should outside intervention be sought. Such violation of confidentiality is justified only after a consumer has steadfastly refused to give permission to act on confidential information.

Although a violation of confidentiality, as well as of self-determination is acceptable when a "super" issue is involved, the question of violation becomes more difficult when the issues become less critical. Suppose, for example, a consumer says he is going to beat someone up. If he said he was going to use a hatchet, a violation of confidentiality might be justified. If the consumer said he was going to use his fists, would a similar violation of confidentiality be justified? How much, how little, what are the consequences? Where and by whom is the line drawn? A definitive response is not possible. Each situation must be evaluated individually and each response determined pragmatically. Intervention in the lives of other people is a most responsible business and must be handled with utmost thought and care. Values are to be neither saluted nor dismissed as substanceless rhetoric; they remain basic to all professional activity. The inherent power in the role of the social worker adds urgency to the attention paid to the value system of social work.

In the interests of efficiency and getting the job done, of trying to keep one's head above a flooded caseload, the principles of confidentiality are often the first to go. To adhere to the concept of confidentiality, the social worker often has to *do* something. The worker may have to ask a consumer to sign something or call up a consumer to request permission or spend valuable time discussing an action that ultimately the consumer will agree to. It is much easier, of course, to simply give the information that is requested over the phone to the other agency. When the information is finally transmitted, *then* something has been done, the "case" has "moved." The process of permission gathering seems to show no discernible result. Red tape, perhaps. Super professionalism. The rationalizations are manifold: "There is no 'problem' here"—"I have more important things to do"—"The consumer is too confused to deal with this"—"He would be initially resistant to change, but it will work out for his good in the long run." The excuses pile up. "After all, don't all social workers work for the best interests of the consumer—all the time?" Although this response is not malicious, confidentiality is nevertheless often sacrificed to "more important" priorities, and each violation distorts the professional role.

Adhering to the letter but violating the spirit of the value, some agencies secure signatures from consumers at the outset for what amounts to a surrender of all rights to confidentiality. It was a common practice at hospitals, of course, during the admission procedure when patients are confused, frightened, and not sure of the possible consequences if they fail to sign. In hospitals where urgent medical matters are often critical, more important issues than confidentiality may very well be at stake. Whereas life and death may take precedence in the hospital situation, the need of patients to recognize their rights and options is in no way diminished; permission must be sought and granted for various procedures. Other persons can be involved with patients at only their request. A social worker who approaches a patient in a hospital and says "May I sit down and talk with you?" is not only recognizing but reaffirming the personal and fundamental rights of the patient. Regardless of the medical priority argument, it remains the task of the social worker to keep patients apprised of the situation and to help patients maintain their rights here as well. When such a situation occurs, the social worker could very easily become an advocate for the patient, particularly when the patient is unable to act on his or her own behalf. As *advocate*, the social worker represents the patient to the hospital authorities.

The social worker also has the responsibility of informing the patient as to what rights to confidentiality she or he really has. The temptation *not* to inform a patient about rights and privileges is sometimes very great, for it gives the worker more time to concentrate on the issues that "really matter." Failure to inform involves a benign neglect that is far reaching. The personal autonomy of the consumer must be recognized by the social worker (as well as others), no matter what the institution, the agency, or the setting in which professional interaction takes place.

In more primitive (and more punitive) times, the threat of disclosure was used as a weapon against people in need. Being dependent, in need of help, was morally reprehensible, tantamount to commission of a crime and punished by forfeiture of the right to privacy, for both the names and addresses of public charges were published in local newspapers. Private matters became public issues. Threatened with violation of their privacy, the poor thought twice about acknowledging their need.

In today's society where technology permits easy access to all private lives, the issue of privacy and confidentiality has become increasingly important. Governmental violations of "confidential" matters reached alarming proportions during the Vietnam War and peaked in the Watergate trauma. The confidentiality of the mails, income tax reports, telephone conversations, voting records, sexual practices, and privacy of domicile were profoundly violated. It raised with renewed concern the question of the existing "rights" of the individual in a postindustrial democratic society.

Respect for the individual—his dignity, his right of self-determination, his right to privacy—is the cornerstone of professional social work. A belief and adherence to these professional values must be rooted deep in social work practice. If the basic value system is adhered to, if the consumer is treated with the dignity and respect to which he is entitled, even in failure there is success, for in the consumer/worker contact, the consumer receives a positive experience.

CHANGING VALUES

A Systems Approach to Social Work

The Informal System. Throughout the history of man, the family unit has remained the basic organizational structure designed to meet personal needs. Traditionally, it is the place to go with hurts, problems, and weariness, as well as with joys and accomplishments. The family nourishes the living and mourns the dying. Even though the family role has waxed and waned during the evolution of man, its essential primacy has allowed it to continue as *the* nourishing unit of life. By extending the nuclear family concept (mother, father, and children) to include close friends and close relatives, the primal, or *informal*, system of social welfare has been identified. Historically, the informal system is the first place where help is sought. Problems of survival, health, child rearing, marriage, and work and career are dealt with principally within the family structure, within the informal system. In the more primitive stages of man, the informal system was the *only* place where relief could be found. The survival needs of the early food gatherers (as opposed to the later food growers) were so great that all activity was directed toward group survival. It was only within the informal system that individual matters of health and welfare could be resolved.

As human society evolved from food gatherers to food growers, revolutionary changes in living patterns emerged that profoundly affected social living. With the development of agriculture and the non-nomadic existence it afforded its practitioners, surplus food became a reality. Food could be grown and food could be stored; the constant activity to secure food for survival lessened. Leisure time became available and, in turn, ushered in issues of "welfare" that transcended physical survival. The ability of the informal system to cope with the problems at hand was challenged as life-styles began to differ. Art, for example, was an activity that had no utilitarian end; relationships between people became more complex. And later, as the machine transformed the world from an agrarian into an industrialized society, even greater complexities challenged the informal system. Values underwent major upheavals, living became even more varied, and what was once a life determined became a life of choice.

Although the informal system has survived the major revolutions in man's evolvement, its ability to meet newer welfare needs effectively is limited. Many people today, for example, are unable to explore a sexual problem within the confines of the informal system. Similarly, the ability to cope with the loss of a job in contemporary society may be beyond the informal system; the economy as a whole is too large a unit for an individual family to significantly influence.

In a preindustrialized agrarian society education occurred in the home. Today, it is almost universally recognized that no informal system has the ability to properly prepare a child for living in contemporary society. And in health care, as well, the family doctor himself has to rely on the expertise of others and on the technologies of health institutions in order to provide necessary services.

Although the services of the informal system remain basic— and essential—they are no longer able to respond completely to the ever-growing complexity of the needs of its members. The future seems to indicate a continued erosion of the informal system and a correspondingly increased reliance on other systems for the services necessary for survival.

The Formal System. Simply stated, the formal system is voluntarily joined in order to ensure survival. Church membership, for example, is part of the formal system. It meets religious or social needs that the informal system is no longer able to satisfy. Also included in the formal system are such organizations as labor unions, Boy and Girl Scouts, fellowship groups (Elks, Odd Fellows, Masons), special-interest groups (NAACP, Sierra Club, the Clamshell Alliance), voluntary hospital plans, and so on. A bridge club is joined to improve playing skills or for companionship; a voluntary hospital plan to ensure adequate medical coverage in the event of chronic or catastrophic illness, a burial group to ensure proper burial, a credit union for a money supply, a union for job protection, and AA for help with a drinking problem. Although the formal and informal systems are obviously interrelated, the existence of the formal system is a recognition of the failure of the informal system to completely meet changing human needs. The *formal* (or voluntary) system supplements the *informal* system. In contemporary society the formal system is the place to go next when the informal system cannot or will not provide the necessary resources.

However, even the formal system may not be sufficient to meet the needs brought to its attention. As a voluntary system, it may be rejected by many people who choose not to join. Some people perhaps do not meet the qualifications for membership, others are unable to gain access to the system, and some are simply unaware of the benefits of the system.

Like the informal system, the resources of the formal network are also limited. They are not, nor can they be, geared to meet all contemporary problems. An unemployed person, for example, may be entitled through union membership to certain benefits for a certain length of time. When those benefits run out, that person must seek extended unemployment benefits provided by a different type of service, a service sponsored by a system larger in scope, resources, and control. But the problems that caused the loss of employment, reflecting the larger social and economic forces in operation, cannot be addressed by the formal system.

A case of child abuse will further illustrate the inadequacy of the formal system. An alcoholic father abuses his child when he is intoxicated. The mother, burdened with the care of her other children, is too overwhelmed to stem these episodic assaults. The informal system obviously cannot resolve the problem, but neither can the formal system because the father refuses to join AA and the mother is too frightened to voluntarily seek services. Another service system needs to be employed.

The Societal Resource System. Intervention in a preventative or a resolution sense must often be sought on the level known as the *societal resource system.* In the societal resource system the energies and resources of the society itself are (or can be) enjoined to meet human service needs.

The societal resource system is the ultimate response to the social welfare needs of the people. Although interrelated with the informal and formal systems, it represents a more comprehensive interventionist level. The extent and direction of the societal resource system is predicated on time and place. It may have been radical to promote regulations governing the employment of children in mines and factories in the nineteenth century, but such legislation is commonplace and unquestioned in today's world.

How society applies its resources, what place the welfare of its citizens occupies in the allocation of its resources, is obviously a large topic. Although it may be naively assumed that the welfare of the people is the essential business of a government, what the term "welfare" actually includes then becomes subject to speculative definition, for, conceivably, military hardware and farm supports for the tobacco crop could be identified as pertinent to the welfare of the people.

In this postindustrial revolutionary world the needs of people continue to multiply, and with the increasing availability of resources to meet those needs, the societal resource system has assumed a greater and more significant role in the lives of people.

The costs of medical care, for example, are often beyond the capability of both the informal and the formal system. Access to medical insurance is often limited to the independently wealthy and the employed. Although the health needs of the indigent and the elderly are met through medicaid and medicare, a total societal resource intervention program to deal with the contemporary health problems of all citizens has yet to be formulated.

The postindustrial, computerized society of today has apparently created more problems for more people and, consequently, an ever-increasing utilization of governmental systems. As more and more new needs emerge, more and more institutions and more and more complex organizations rise to meet those needs, all pointing to a greater deployment of societal resource systems. Even so, the societal resource systems in the United States still lag behind the services provided by other industrialized nations.

It is within these three interrelated systems that social work flourishes. Although less visible at times in the informal system, part of social work's task has been the perpetuation and development of the informal system. Traditionally seen as the basic ingredient to a fruitful and satisfying life, the informal system, that is, within the nuclear family, often provides the best hope for the resolution of certain problems that fall within its province. Values, however, are shifting and with the proliferation of societal resource systems and the growing recognition of *rights* rather than *privileges*, the future of the informal system may someday be seriously questioned. At the present time, however, the bonds and services of the family and close friends are seen as those strengths that must be built upon first and foremost to enhance the quality of living.

Social work is more visible in the formal system of private and voluntary social welfare agencies, which are strongly linked to societal resource systems through funding and sanction. And finally, in the public service agencies of the societal resource systems social work has played a traditionally prominent role.

THREE

THE WAY
IT WORKS

THE SERVICE DELIVERY
SYSTEM

The service delivery system is a network of social service systems—child-welfare system, mental-health system, corrections, welfare and medical systems, and so on—designed to meet specific needs. Within the systems are smaller units, the social agencies, that provide the resources and procedures to service those needs. Agencies are linked both horizontally with other agencies performing related services and vertically with regulatory agencies above, which set guidelines for such services, and perhaps with satellite agencies below. These linkages acknowledge a public and private mandate to provide such social services. The social worker is employed by the agency to deliver the service to the individual consumer.

THE AGENCY

The Limits of Practice

The agency sanctions the service performed by social workers. Within the agency structure, a social worker's practice is limited by legal, quasi-legal, and conditional regulations. As no single agency can possibly offer unlimited service to unlimited populations, every agency limits its operations to specific areas. Limits may be determined by the nature of the problems that the agency chooses to address. For example, a community decides that services for teen-agers take precedence over services to the aged. Services consequently focus on the establishment of a Y, for example, rather than a Golden Age club. The elderly in that community are directed to other service agencies for attention. Even multiservice centers where many types of service are offered under one roof do not escape limitations to their purview. Thus, a community mental health center must still limit its service to the problem "area" of mental health.

Limits may also be determined by the availability of an agency's resources, its funds, the size of its physical plant, the numbers of its staff, and even by the predilections of its advisory board. Private agencies obviously have greater choice, whereas the services of public agencies are legally mandated.

Similar agencies often use geographical boundaries, so-called catchment areas, to determine the physical limits of their services. Hospitals, for example, deal with the medical problems of a population living within a specific geographical catchment area. Certain agencies, however, serve only a designated number of people—limited by money, staff, or even by design—rather than a designated catchment area.

Public social service delivery systems, such as the Department of Welfare or the Human Services Administration, offer an extraordinarily wide range of social services. The Department of Welfare rarely denies service on the basis of insufficient numbers of social workers or a shortage of funds. Consumers are denied service only when they fail to meet the stated eligibility requirements. Conversely, private agencies can pick and choose. The administrators of a private mental hospital, for example, can refuse to admit a consumer they consider too ill to benefit from service. A public hospital, however, must admit the consumer regardless of the severity of the illness.

Agencies are further limited by their practice standards, which vary from agency to agency and are determined by not only the nature of the service but also the agency's philosophy of service. The professional standards taught by universities and codified by the professional society are often at variance with agency practice. The policies of agency governing boards, the attitudes of the community, and regulation by other agencies often reflect points of view other than those of the profession. Inevitably, then, there is a distance between professional standards and agency practice. In order to be satisfactorily employed, the social worker must be comfortable with that distance.

The social worker, for example, in a correctional system is bound by practice standards that reflect the philosophy of the uniformed staff, which includes containment, control, punishment as a therapeutic tool, and discipline, whereas in a family agency the practice philosophy, essentially benign, endeavors to help a family understand communication problems and to "work through" personal difficulties. And again, within an agency, regardless of its orientation, the organizational needs of the service usually infringe on the ideal practice standards, for social work practice is essentially a compromise between professional ideals and the actual working realities of the agency.

An agency sometimes makes demands, in the interest of operational efficiency, that are not in strict accordance with the needs of a particular consumer. To ensure efficiency, a certain amount of uniformity in policy in regard to the allocation of limited resources and in recognition of the necessity of compromise between professional and nonprofessional points of view is required.

The discrepancy between institutional needs and individual consumer needs is easily illustrated in a residential treatment setting. Children are "placed" in a residential treatment setting voluntarily by parents and nonvoluntarily by courts for reasons of emotional disturbance or acts of delinquency. The children "live" at these residences twenty-four hours a day. To select one example among many, residential treatment settings must determine a policy on home visiting: When does a child spend time at home and under what circumstances? To maximize agency efficiency, a uniform policy of home visiting is most advantageous. An efficient home visiting procedure can be structured to provide a bus for cottage A one week, cottage B the next, and so on. From the social worker's point of view, however, a home visit is best determined by the individual needs of the particular child and family. Visiting is not uniform and is subject to individual situations and circumstances. Some children prefer going home every weekend, others hardly at all. Although this procedure produces more administrative turmoil, it nevertheless better serves the needs of the children. From an administrative point of view, an ever-changing home visiting policy means advance planning is difficult, weekend staffing is confusing, agency costs are increased, and increased costs, in turn, prevent the addition of another social worker to the staff. And residents, not knowing whether they are going or staying, are more disruptive.

Conflict between the needs of an agency to ensure efficient operation and the needs of the consumer is inevitable. Not necessarily "bad," conflict is rather a reality of agency practice. Social workers must be prepared to deal with this compromise.

Referral. When a consumer appears at a halfway house for mental patients to seek help in securing money to pay the rent, an obvious referral to the Department of Welfare is in order, unless, of course, the consumer is a former resident of the halfway house and the financial need is indicative of a previous mental condition. A less obvious situation may require some investigation before the nature of the problem is fully recognized, at which time referral is made. Often consumers are simply unaware of the services available. Sometimes an agency provides the service of preparing a consumer for referral to a more appropriate agency. Working with a nonvoluntary consumer in a parole situation may prepare him to accept a referral to a voluntary agency where a more specialized service may be available, to a local Y, for example, or a community mental health center.

Referral is a most important service. Because service delivery systems are so narrowly defined, the extent and breadth of the resource landscape in the United States is staggering. Although recent movements toward comprehensive service agencies that offer a variety of services under one roof allow referral to be made to other divisions within the agency, much investigative work is nevertheless often required before the proper referral can be made. Resource expertness is necessary to be fully aware of what does and what does not exist in the area of resources— where to get them and how to get them—and a considerable amount of time is often required to link a consumer with the appropriate service delivery system.

Referral is not simply a matter of providing a consumer with an address and travel directions to another agency. Feelings are involved with going from one service to another. A consumer may be reluctant or embarrassed to use an available resource for personal reasons, such as a poor previous experience with that service. An informed worker can often make the transition to a new agency easier for a consumer by informing him completely about the services provided by the new agency. And, with the consumer's permission, a phone call to the new agency to summarize the worker's contact with the consumer may also smooth the transition and be of considerable service to both the consumer and the receiving agency.

In addition to knowing where, and how, to get services, the

worker must consider the consumer's eligibility. Many agencies require voluntarism on the part of the consumer as a prerequisite for service. Many mental health services, for example, require a consumer to acknowledge the existence of the problem and indicate a willingness to participate in the helping process. Alcoholics Anonymous is another example.

Referral to an inappropriate agency or a distortion of the services provided are serious mistakes. Knowledge of an agency is not simply an understanding of the services of an agency and the means of access, but also its eligibility requirements, its intake policy, and its waiting list. Sending a consumer to an agency whose waiting list numbers in the hundreds is not going to help that consumer a great deal.

In short, the referral procedure invokes the same configuration that is required in consumer/worker professional interactions.

Knowing the Agency

A solid grasp of the organization, structure, and operational methods of the agency is basic to effective practice. The purposes of the agency and the strengths and limitations of its service must be identified and understood by the social worker in order to realistically negotiate with a consumer for service. As part of a service delivery system, the extent of the social worker's operations is determined by that system. Workers recognize and acknowledge that they are offering not only themselves and their skills but also the agency and the agency's resources, as well as linkages to other service networks.

An intimate knowledge of agency resources, that is, specific services available to support the social worker or those directly available to the consumer, is essential. The extent and kind of agency resources available reflect the nature of the problems with which the agency is concerned. They also reflect the direction of the agency, that is, the agency's approach to service delivery. For example, a family agency may offer any number of approaches to dealing with problems of the family. An agency may work either with various family members individually, with the family as a distinct constellation, or with groups consisting of separate families, such as a "fathers' group," a "mothers' group," or a parents' group. Agencies may offer various combinations of these. An agency's approach also reflects its bias toward one of the current psychological theories, such as a psychoanalytic, a behavioral, or a gestalt approach to family dynamics. All of this combines to lend a distinctive character to the particular agency.

In a small agency, information regarding agency resources is relatively easy to obtain. In a large agency, however, such as a public agency or a large private agency, such information may be quite difficult to obtain and require considerable time to fully comprehend.

The needs of any individual or group cannot be met in isolation. Only the combined resources of an agency, both its material and its immaterial supports, can provide the needed service. The more experienced social worker is quite aware of the advantages of this combined effort. Beginning workers, however, concerned about revealing their lack of knowledge or skills, may attempt to handle situations on their own and thus fail to capitalize on available supports.

The social worker's task is to provide service not only to the consumer but to the agency itself, so that better and more effective service can be made available to all the consumers being served by the agency. This might be accomplished by developing new resources or, perhaps, new directions in service delivery.

As the social worker is part of an agency system, so is the agency part of a larger system of service delivery. Each agency is part of an overall network of agencies. How they operate with one another—the nature of their linkage, their mutuality or exclusivity, the complementarity of their services—is essential information that allows the social worker and the consumer to seek out the best way to deal with specific problems. Knowledge of related agencies, their services, and their methods of operation is, of course, essential to properly refer a consumer for additional services or to enable a worker to call on the resources of other agencies to help the consumer. In the process of referral, the social worker helps the consumer to "negotiate" the various systems of service.

The priorities of a particular agency and its methods of service delivery are largely determined by the secondary service systems. The nature of the work that transpires between social worker and consumer, in turn, is largely determined by the agency. By examining the various systems that impact on a consumer, the social worker can direct the consumer to the most appropriate agency based on his understanding of the mutually interacting systems. Through an understanding of the larger systems of service, social workers are in a better position to improve the quality or increase the quantity of the offered service.

As a member of an agency, as opposed to private practice, the worker is better able to induce broader social change, for an agency's resources are far greater than those of an individual social worker. For example, if the worker discerns a needed service in the community that the agency can provide, he or she has access to the power strucure that can implement that service. Part friend, part enemy, the agency system can best serve the needs of people when it is best understood.

To be a successful practitioner, the social worker must understand agency organization and structure. In reality, the agency social worker has two clients, the consumer and the agency itself. To ensure satisfaction of the consumer's needs, the social worker must work to improve the structure of the service delivery system.

Often the social worker finds that the agency, like the consumer, is resistant to change.

WHAT A SOCIAL WORKER DOES

Social work provides either *direct* or *indirect* services to people.

Direct service refers to a face-to-face contact with a person in need of service. The social worker, the visible helping agent, performs the service. *Indirect* service, which is less visible, refers to work that does not involve direct consumer contact, that is, the work of supervisors, administrators, coordinators, program evaluators, fund raisers, lobbyists, researchers, consultants, teachers, and so on.

Direct service is subdivided into direct service: concrete and direct service: supportive.

Direct Service: Concrete

The delivery of specific services, easily identifiable and tangible, such as finding a job for a consumer, locating an apartment, providing food stamps, money, material goods, and information, is called the delivery of *concrete services*. Other examples include finding a nursing home, providing a tutor, referring to another system, providing carfare, filling out medicaid forms, and taking a child for an ice-cream soda.Providing concrete services was a prime function of early social workers in the United States. The work of the friendly visitors and the acts of charity and of ''welfare'' throughout the early years was, for the most part, concrete in nature. Also offered were non-concrete efforts to improve the ''character'' of the recipients of the public largesse through the use of uplifting lectures, the use of fear (punishment, shame, degradation), guilt, religion, and moralizing. There was also a not-so-hidden assumption that "character" would improve through the emulation of their "betters" (i.e., the people who delivered the services).

Providing concrete service, still the major and most essential task of social work, requires professional skills for effective delivery. With the development of professional schools, as mentioned earlier, the "direction" of social work tended to move away from concrete services and toward emotional supportive services. The public agencies, the prime deliverers of concrete services, had to look elsewhere for staffing as school-trained social workers moved to private agencies where supportive work was emphasized. Today social workers with BSW degrees provide the major concrete services, and supportive services are staffed by social workers with advanced training.

Direct Service: Supportive

Commonly known as "therapeutic" service, *supportive service* is concerned with the emotional and psychological problems of the consumer. Less tangible and more difficult to identify and describe than concrete services, supportive service is nevertheless concerned with a vital human factor—feelings. Readily recognized as a common human factor, feelings govern the quality and choice of activities, life-styles, and even perceptions of the world.

A social worker cannot help a consumer if the worker is unaware of the consumer's feelings in relation to his current life situation. Feelings are tremendously important regardless of whether the consumer is searching for a larger apartment for his family or is working on intense problems of sexual identification. Whether the service rendered is basically supportive or basically concrete depends on emphasis. As work on a concrete problem without regard to "feelings" would be irresponsible, so work on an emotional problem without regard to the real objects that provoke the emotions would be equally irresponsible.

Providing concrete services requires a knowledge of community resources and services of agencies and procedures. Supportive services require such far less tangible factors as empathy, sensitivity, and self-awareness. The worker's task is to "get in touch" with the consumer's feelings, for by getting to know the "feeling" world of the consumer, the worker is able to help the consumer within the world.

Pity is not supportive. Neither are such stock phrases as, "I understand what you are going through," "I understand what you feel." Effective supportive work requires a sensitivity in the real sense of the word. It is only by sincerely listening to the consumer, by "tuning in" to his feelings, by treating his feelings with the utmost respect, caution, and consideration—even alien or distasteful feelings—that the worker can realistically help the consumer.

The setting one works in, the problems being dealt with, and to some extent the skills of the social worker determine the extent and the nature of the work. Supportive services may go beyond a recognition of feelings, empathy, and ego support. In some situations it may be appropriate for the social worker to help the consumer sort out his feelings, expand his awareness of them, deal with his counterproductive ambivalences, trace his feelings to their roots, and alleviate the accompanying guilt and anxiety. A general understanding of feelings and how they operate is essential to the practice of social work. How to work with feelings will be discussed later.

Supervision. Because of the enormous number of factors that the social worker must deal with daily, supervision is essential. Considering all the issues that combine in a worker/consumer interaction, no one special worker, no matter how skilled, could possibly sort them all into a meaningful content. By consulting with a skilled and objective outsider—the supervisor—the worker can ensure a professional approach. When the worker "cannot see the forest for the trees"—caught up in the myriad details of a worker/consumer interaction—the grand plan, the thrust of the work itself may become obscure. By identifying the purpose and direction of the work and ensuring that it is progressing in accordance with professional agency standards, the supervisor can bring the "forest" into focus. For example, resistance, or barriers, in the worker/consumer interaction is to be expected. The supervisor from his or her perspective can help the worker identify barriers and suggest ways through which these barriers can be overcome. Social work practice is openended. A social worker is in the continuous process of becoming a better social worker. Skills can be improved, techniques can be reevaluated, and a deeper understanding and greater knowledge can be sought. The supervisor can help in pursuing these goals.

The social worker is primarily concerned with the individual consumer, family, or group with whom he or she is working. The worker's next priority is his or her aggregate of consumers, the caseload, that is, how to manage all the cases with which he or she is involved, how to allocate time, and so on. Under normal circumstances, the essential focus of a worker's endeavor is the direct service for which he or she is primarily responsible. To the supervisor and to the agency, the social worker is the principal advocate for the consumers he or she is serving.

Similarly, the supervisor is the principal advocate to the agency for the social workers he or she is serving. In addition to supervising the social workers, the supervisor has the responsibility of communicating to the agency the service needs of the social workers. As the advocate of the agency to the worker, the supervisor interprets administrative policies and directives to the direct service staff and monitors the implementation of the agency's policies and directives.

The supervisor views the social worker in relationship to the consumer and in relationship to the other social workers in the agency. The supervisor also judges the effectiveness of the worker in delivering service. The allocation of a supervisor's time—for teaching, supervising, training—is determined by the needs of the workers and the standards of performance expected. The supervisor is aware of the details of the agency and has access to the wider system of resources. The supervisor's wider view of the service needs and resources of the whole agency allows a realistic distribution of these resources. A priority system is necessary for successful case management. Not everything can be done with equal devotion at the same time. A range of "urgencies"—from "emergency" or "crisis" to "irksome" or "minor"—is required.

THE CONSUMER SYSTEM

The *consumer system* includes the family system, the human physiological and psychological systems, the racial and religious systems, the environmental system, the cultural, employment, and social systems. The consumer is in constant interaction with this complex network of systems, which are, in turn, interacting with each other. At a given point in time, all or one of these systems may trouble a consumer and cause him or her to seek assistance.

The service delivery system and the consumer system meet in the initial encounter to determine whether a basis exists for these two systems to be involved with each other. If such a basis exists, the worker and the consumer determine the extent of the contract. If no basis exists, the consumer is referred to the proper agency.

FOUR

PREPARING FOR SOCIAL WORK

Social work can be identified as the *application* of all that is known and understood and all that can be inferred to working with people to help them understand themselves and their environments. Social work practice, however, does not consist of a series of discrete studied and learned responses. Instead, it must be viewed as a process like the flow of a river that changes course to accommodate its environment and at the same time remains true to its characterization as a river. The reality of the setting, the agency structure and function, the social problems identified, the populations concerned, and the methods of intervention authorized determine to an enormous extent the practice. There remains, however, an underlying uniformity in social work practice that permits the worker to function regardless of the setting.

ESTABLISHING A BALANCE

Social work demands a unique combination of knowledge and skills fused in such a way as to most efficiently satisfy conflicting conditions.

Social work must establish a balance between providing services to people to improve the quality of their lives and at the same time not interfere with their rights to live their lives in accordance with their own standards and ideals. In other words, to provide service that respects a consumer's right to self-determination. A balance must also be established between resources and needs. A social worker can introduce only a limited amount of resources to meet what is often unlimited need. Resources—money, clothing, food, time, support, and knowledge—are limited. All too often the consumer's needs (or demands) exceed the existing resources. Not even the best psychotherapy can "cure" neurotic problems; such therapy can only resolve such problems to allow the consumer to resume functioning. For many situations, then, even unlimited resources cannot fully satisfy existing needs. The social worker, the ultimate pragmatist, must constantly find ways to balance people's needs with existing resources.

The service provided to the consumer must be neither too much nor too little. Too little service, obviously, is inadequate, a denial of the avowed purpose of social work. But too much service is also counterproductive. Too much service tends to make consumers *too* needful of the social worker's services or *too* dependent on the resources of the agency, which, in turn, deprives consumers of their right to growth, independence, and decision making. The "art" of social work lies in the effective balancing of the constant opposites that social workers encounter.

Social Work as Practice. Social work training is designed to meaningfully combine a sequence of knowledge and skills, that is, to provide a combination of information, values, and skills, that will enable the social worker to carry out assignments most effectively. Actually, however, social work requires more than simply knowledge and skill. It is a discipline that requires the translation of knowledge and skills into direct work with people, that is, knowledge and skills must become operational. The essence of social work lies in the direct *practice* of social work with people.

No "Complete" Answers. Beginning social workers often experience frustration when they realize that they are not being taught specific answers to the questions they will encounter in the field. The realities of working with people in the vast social landscape serve only to identify the lack of knowledge of human beings and their environment and force the social worker to the painful acknowledgment that all the answers are not yet known.

The fantasy that beginning social workers often have about social work—its inherent ability to solve problems—is quickly shattered in the real world. As reality creeps stealthily in and dramatic cures and hairbreadth rescues are not forthcoming, the beginning social worker realizes that social work is difficult and painstaking; its progress is more often measured in millimeters than in bounding leaps. Although workers hope for radical changes for the better, they are forced, all too often, to learn to accept moderate changes, status quo situations, even simply the halt of declining situations. At times, there is failure.

When the initial expectations and fantasies of student social workers begin to fizzle out, they sometimes begin to realize that their desire to help people change their lives for the better is grandiose. An encounter with a skilled social worker, an encounter best measured in a limited series of hours, cannot be expected to remake a human being or undo the years of bad experience that prompted the current problem.

Change frequently, when it does come, comes too slowly. Real changes, insightful interventions do occur; constructive intervention generates enthusiasm and stimulates activities that can be extremely beneficial. But a stark assessment of the realities with which social workers must contend and the limited knowledge and resources with which they have to work can be discouraging. The social worker hopes for pertinent intervention and at the same time recognizes the realities of living, the realities that behavior is often difficult to modify; that life in society exists imperfectly, that imbalances and injustices in the allocation and distribution of resources are often insurmountable. The task of the social worker, then, must be to help people cope with the imperfections of contemporary life. Often the social worker must deal with only symptom alleviation, for people must be able to cope in the here and now; the opportunity to alleviate causal problems is frequently limited. Racism, endemic problems of unemployment, inadequate services and resources for any given social problem, a budget of bare subsistence, the humiliations of welfare procedure, illnesses, and handicaps—these are the realities. A social worker can only hope to help people recognize and cope with their own particular realities.

Until recently, questions of causation were infrequently addressed. Today, however, the problems of consumers are more apt to be viewed from the comprehensive perspective of social, cultural, economic, and familial systems, as well as from a psychological systems perspective, which had formerly been the social worker's chief instrument of assessment. It is this holistic concept of causation that determines how the social worker will intervene in any given situation. Assessing problems from a multilevel point of view modifies practice stances. Working more with the person in the community rather than in the confines of the agency office is one example. The searching out of problems before they reach unmanageable "crisis" proportions points to new directions for social workers. Developing preventative services, teaching, consulting, and developing impacting techniques in community environments indicate the expansionist direction toward which social work is now moving.

The tools to resolve all the problems of people are only in their formative stages. Until they are perfected, the reality of social work represents only small steps toward that goal.

Relevancy of Knowledge. Students are often agonizingly frustrated when they discover that their knowledge, by itself, is not sufficient to meet the task at hand. Knowledge and information must not only be learned and understood conceptually, it must be *applied* directly to the work; it must be relevant to what the social worker does.

A social worker, for example, may have a good idea as to why a child is having a temper tantrum. To take this understanding and put it to work for the consumer, to make this knowledge applicable, to make it operational is the true art of social work.

As the larger emerging roles of the social worker are further developed, the use of knowledge and expertise to accomplish desired social ends will extend to the newer "consumer," that is, community leaders, members of the power structure, peers, professionals, paraprofessionals, and ordinary citizens as well as the traditional "consumer," the welfare recipient, the elderly, the physically and mentally ill, the addict, the foster child, the disturbed child, and so on.

From Knowledge to Relevancy. The need to translate knowledge into practice requires that the education of the social worker take place in two distinct arenas: the university and the agency.

In the classroom the student is taught the essential intellectual content of social work—the cultural, environmental, and psychological systems, the values of social work, and theoretical and conceptual material—as well as basic professional skills. The knowledge thus gained is put to work in another environment, known as an *agency* in particular and the *field* in general. The field is the arena where the providers and the receivers of the benefits of social work meet. It is in the field that the student faces the reality of social work life, working with people on a face-to-face basis.

The student social worker is assigned to a field agency that meets the professional practice standards as defined by the school. The student works under the close guidance of a field instructor, an experienced social worker, whose knowledge and competency have also been evaluated by the school. The field instructor provides the work experience for the student social worker. As mentioned earlier, the specific assignments are determined by the nature of the agency, the problems it elects to deal with, and its consumer population, as well as by the agency's philosophy of service provision. Cases are selected and the field instructor prepares the student to encounter consumers in real situations with real problems. Both the field instructor and the agency make these decisions with care and consideration, aware of the limitations of beginning students as well as the agency's commitment to the consumer. At this important beginning, students are assured that they are not out there to swim alone, that they are expected to learn, and that help is at hand.

The field experience for the student is a synthesizing experience; knowledge and skills are united, and professional values are actualized and incorporated into practice. The student is transformed into the "helping instrument" aspired to. By attempting to put everything into place, the field experience is, at its core, pragmatic. The integration process, however, is a long one, accomplished over a period of time that extends far beyond the educational experience itself, More realistically, it is an experience that extends throughout a social worker's professional life.

THE "HELPING INSTRUMENT" CONCEPT

As must be clear by now, good intentions by themselves do not necessarily make for effective social work. Nor can social work without good intentions be effective. Nor do the knowledge/value base and the skill base by themselves produce good practice. To meet the goal of effective practice, all these elements must be combined in a disciplined manner. Effectiveness is defined as providing maximum service within the professional value context. Without a value context, "effective" service can easily be identified with control and authoritarianism. Values, however, without a mechanism of service delivery become meaningless gestures. Effective professional service requires a balance between service efficiency and values.

In this context it is helpful to think of the social worker as being the "helping instrument." "Helping" in the sense of assisting others as per the mandate of social work, and "instrument" in the sense of discipline, purposefulness, and containment, that is, the use of the self as a "tool" in the provision of human services. The social worker *is* the "helping instrument"; the essential tool of the social worker is the social worker himself.

This concept implies that part of the education of the social worker lies in an understanding of oneself as a person and an ability to consciously use oneself in one's work. Through an awareness of self, one can learn to use oneself in the most constructive manner possible.

Looking Inward. The difficulties students face in schools of social work are not usually of an intellectual nature. For the most part, the intellectual demands appear to be manageable by the majority of student social workers. The frustrations and learning pains that all students experience, to varying degrees, have to do with efforts students must make in *looking inward*.

Looking inward is a process of self-examination in which the student assesses himself or herself as a person, as a personality, as a human being, as a product of a variety of emotional and environmental forces. Looking inward results in a degree of self-understanding, a self-understanding that leads to objectivity in the work situation. When the self-understanding component is combined with the knowledge, skill, and value components of the field, the image of the social worker as a helping instrument comes into sharper focus.

For many students the process of looking inward, of developing self-awareness, can be uncomfortable because it requires an objective examination of one's motives, impulses, and feelings that have often been taken for granted, accepted for being what they are, or avoided as being too frightening to realistically pursue. For those students whose backgrounds include some self-examination, this significant aspect of the professional training can be a stimulating and exciting experience, adding new dimensions of self-awareness. These students should develop not only a more in-depth awareness of self but also control of their feelings in the professional work situation. Control of self is the next step to understanding of self.

For the student who is looking inward with some objectivity for the first time, however, the experience can be alternately frightening and exciting. Frightening because there are always parts of oneself that would best be avoided, exciting because understanding leads to mastery, and mastery of oneself leads to better performance in the field. By recognizing and understanding one's own inner landscape, one is able to capitalize on that understanding to develop more effective skills.

Looking inward is essentially a nonintellectual process. The act itself requires almost a suspension of the intellectual and cognitive parts of the mind so that subjective experiences can surface. Only later can self-awareness be sorted out intellectually and be put to use in practice.

For the student who approaches the world intellectually, the difficulties experienced in looking inward may be keen, for the ability to conceptualize, abstract, reason, and cognitively grasp material is *not* the essential here. Students who are less intellectually endowed but closer to their own selves and feelings may perform somewhat better. The intellectual student, in fact, may be quite upset when he or she discovers for the first time in an educational experience that intellectual expertise does *not* provide easy access.

The practice of social work is not solely intellectual. It requires empathy, awareness, sensitivity—feelings that cannot be reached or developed primarily through intellectual endeavor. But they can be developed. The work experience itself, the mere situational impact of working with other people's feelings must, of necessity, evoke one's own.

This intense process of self-examination is necessary because social work is not simply the manipulation of people. The humanistic value base of the profession assumes there is more to both the givers and receivers of services than their cognitive functions.

Self-awareness. Because the social worker is such an integral part of the service being offered, his or her person, being, and motives must be above reproach. The specific resources—information, goods, expertise, support—must be offered, obviously, in a manner consistent with professional practice standards. If not, such "giving" is self-serving to the social worker and meaningless at best, and possibly harmful at worst, to the consumer. The development of self-awareness permits social workers to understand more completely where they as persons with their own needs, wants, and desires *begin* and *end* and where a consumer's needs, wants, and desires *begin* and *end*. It is only through such understanding that service can be maximized and reflective of the consumer's needs.

The social worker, like other human beings, is a combination of feelings, attitudes, myths, knowledge, fantasies, virtues, hangups, prejudices, absurdities, and all the other qualities that make up the human condition. Even while working, the social worker retains this reservoir of humanness. Trained social workers, unlike most other people, however, are sufficiently aware of themselves in *all* their dimensions to prevent these factors from interfering with the accomplishment of professional tasks. It is this awareness, actually, that enables the social worker to recognize the humanity of the consumer and thus be *better* able to provide service. Understanding oneself and being able to control oneself is the meaning of self-awareness.

Social workers often deal with people in crisis and their encounters are frequently intense. Angry, happy, resentful, frustrated, hostile, sad, depressed, or even extremely ill, consumers need information, reassurance, guidance, a shoulder to cry on, a direction to go in; they may want to share their despair, vent their anger, report an injustice, plead a cause, express a need, or simply scream at the gods. To all these people and to all their needs and wants, the social worker must, somehow, respond.

How one responds depends, to a considerable extent, on one's feelings, one's emotional state, at that given time. When one is happy or excited, time seems to fly. When "feeling good" predominates, the world seems a happier place and people are enjoyable and fun to be with. Problems seem less formidable. On the other hand, when one feels depressed, angry, or unhappy, one also perceives the world as angry and threatening. Problems magnify; even petty annoyances become awesome burdens. During these "down" stages, life itself becomes a painful chore, an endless succession of difficulties and headaches for which there is no discernible relief in sight.

One's prevailing mood filters life experiences, determines how one sees, hears, and feels, and how one reaches out to the world. Although the mood filtration process is obvious during high and low emotional extremes, it is also a factor during even-tempered emotional states. Feelings at any given point in time both influence one's perception of the world and condition one's reaction to it.

Social workers who work intimately with people in stress are confronted not with one filtration process but with two—their own and the consumer's. How much does a social worker perceive the consumer and his world through his own filtration process? How much of the consumer's situation is influenced by his emotional feelings at any given time? The worker must be aware how these subjective states continually influence reality perception.

As human beings, social workers are not computerized recorders nor do they react machinelike, with constant objectivity, to the world. How then can social workers recognize and thus minimize such inherent subjectivity to ensure objective responses to a consumer's problem?

Early in the field experience, the field instructor helps students explore the subjectivity of their own human responses. Students learn to recognize their general feelings about people and to accept their own specific responses to various types of consumers. They are helped generally to become more sensitive to their own feelings through questions and comments from field instructors. A generalized recognition of the role that one's own feelings play in the helping process and a permission to deal with them during the supervisory sessions mark the beginning steps here. Gradually, students become more aware of their own feelings and are able to acknowledge their influence in the work situation.

Through the intervention of the field instructor, students are helped to identify, more specifically, just how subjective needs influence responses to consumers and to understand those qualities in themselves that inevitably intrude in the interaction with others. At this point stress is on a rather gross level of subjective feelings, overall emotional climates that influence one's perceptions of others and will inevitably influence responses to others.

The world outside also influences subjective feelings, which, in turn, influence one's response to that world.

One's initial reaction to another person, for example, is most often triggered by their physical appearance: their sex, skin color, hair color, height, clothes. The social worker may find these particular attributes interesting, exciting, or dull. In social situations one can act upon feelings, walk away from one person, move toward another. In the professional situation, however, this luxury of response is not permitted. People who are in need cannot be accepted or rejected on the basis of one's likes or dislikes, or by one's given emotional mood at the time.

If a social worker's own feelings about a particular consumer are too strong to be contained, the case should be reassigned. It is the mark of the professional to recognize his or her own limitations. Very strong emotional attachments, either positive or negative, that tend to influence objectivity fall into this category.

Conversely, it is not necessary for social workers to love or even like the consumer. But a social worker must *respect* the consumer and be able to work with him or her objectively if a high degree of professional service is to be rendered.

In the consumer/worker relationship an infinite number of emotional reactions are evoked in both the consumer and the worker—memories and associations going back to earlier periods, people and events that have been lived through and reacted to in various ways, emotional responses of likes and dislikes. In the professional encounter, however, social workers must be aware of the range and depth of their responses to consumers' problems.

Social workers' awareness of their own feelings allows them to be more objective and thus more aware of the expressions and needs of consumers, that is, the more social workers are in touch with their own feelings and subjective reactions, the better they are able to relate pertinently to consumers' situations.

Finding oneself in other people is a common occurrence. In

everyday life, people reflect one another and respond accordingly. Generally, one does not like people who exhibit qualities that one is trying to hide in oneself. For example, the "macho" man who overreacts to the homosexual's approach by beating him up, the homosexual here reflecting the macho's own hidden desires. This uncomfortable recognition is, although it is perhaps not too obvious, one of the reasons for one's dislike of others. One person may be "too competitive," another "too passive," reflecting areas that one is struggling with. By the same token, one usually likes people who reflect those qualities most liked in oneself.

A consumer's problems often parallel the social worker's and in these situations the worker may respond in terms of his or her own needs rather than those of the consumer. For example, the mother of a relatively new worker in a social agency, hospitalized for a severe illness, is now ready for discharge. Faced with the choice of placing her in a nursing home until she recovers fully or having her live with him for a period of time, the social worker decides, after much consideration, that a nursing home is best for both his mother and himself. It is not an easy decision. The new worker's caseload includes a consumer whose father has been living with her and her family for some time. Now he is getting older, becoming more of a burden, producing friction in the home. What should she do?

The initial tendency of the new social worker is to "advise" placement in the nursing home. Consider the advantages from the social worker's point of view. He would not be alone in placing a parent outside the home. "Look, sometimes we have to do this, as painful as this may be." The symbolic sharing of guilt, a collective guilt (*everyone* is doing this terrible thing), is easier to bear than individual guilt ("I'm the only one in the world guilty of this heinous act"). The social worker marshals all the arguments he used to buttress his own decision, emphasizing the factors favoring placement in a nursing home and minimizing the factors favoring the old man's remaining at the consumer's home. With something "at stake" in the consumer's decision making, the social worker can easily slant his responses to influence the consumer. Obviously, this is not social work of the highest order. Rather, the consumer must be given the opportunity to explore her options free from the biases of the social worker.

Self-awareness can help avoid these rather obvious pitfalls. For the new social worker, attention to these subjective concerns comes from the field instructor or the supervisor. All social workers at one time or another fall into these subjective traps. When it occurs, it should be not an embarrassing experience but a learning experience. In the process of helping human beings, *their* needs and *their* perceptions of the world remain paramount.

Having *complete* control of one's feelings, it may be argued, can lead to a distortion, a clinical automaton who responds coldly and impassively to all people and events. The control of one's feelings and subjective reactions, however, does not mean that these feelings automatically disappear, but only that they be used constructively. For example, the social worker who reaches out and holds a frightened child is obviously responding with feelings of warmth and concern and in the process is permitting some of his or her own feelings to be used constructively. The social worker, however, giving vent to anger toward the mother who abused her child is *not* helping the mother—condemnation never leads to reform—but is responding to the situation from his or her own vantage point. And any possibility of a meaningful relationship between the consumer and the social worker is, of course, gone forever.

Feelings, then, must be controlled, not always suppressed, not always vented. The significant question is: Whose needs are being satisfied by the social worker's reactions? The consumer's? The worker's own? Honest answers to these questions often involve painful soul-searching. If one's own needs are being met, they must be resolved elsewhere, by one's supervisor, one's friends, or by confronting oneself. If a subjective reaction to any given situation is to be used in the work, it must be used to serve the consumer.

Personal Therapy: Yes or No? Being aware of emotional problems and resolving personal problems are two different things. In order for a social worker to practice, only the former is required *as long as the worker's personal problems do not interfere with the work.* As long as social workers can exercise sufficient control over their problems so that their helpfulness and objectivity are not subverted, they can be effective practitioners.

When a worker's emotional problems surface in the work, however, questions can legitimately be raised. The supervisor must locate the difficulty, identify it, and help the worker (or student) to deal with it. But it is not the supervisor's (or field instructor's) job to help the social worker solve the problem. The supervisor is concerned not with the cause of the problem but with its manifestation in the work. The distinction between supervision and therapy may be difficult for the beginning social worker to make. Work-related problems are fair game for the supervisor, who is instrumental in helping the worker deal with or control such problems *in the work.*

If a social worker's personal problems continually spill over into the work, therapeutic intervention may be needed. If not, then a personal therapeutic experience is not indicated for that reason. However, because an understanding of oneself is of enormous help in the understanding of others, a worker's therapeutic experience can be extremely beneficial.

In psychotherapeutic agencies where the social worker engages in an intimate process with the consumer that includes establishing intricate relationships and dealing with intensive emotional questions and potent transference and countertransference issues, a social worker's own psychotherapeutic experience is almost required.

In addition to the technical considerations, for workers to engage in therapy without undergoing therapy themselves is a denial of a process. It is a way for workers to separate themselves from the common mold, a way to reiterate the myth that workers have no problems, only consumers have problems. Social workers who engage in psychotherapeutic practice without having experienced the process themselves retain an arrogance that can only hinder, not help.

The search for self-awareness may force students to face themselves squarely and sometimes painfully. What they see and experience may raise important personal questions, may present issues that need further exploration. Issues under control in the private self may emerge painfully in the professional self. The resolution of one's own problems often increases one's awareness of other people's problems and enables the worker to develop additional helping skills.

Therapy, for the social worker, however, must remain an option, not a requirement. It is a decision individuals must make for themselves.

BEYOND EMPATHY—A CLIMATE OF POSSIBLE CHANGE

Beyond empathy, the social worker must offer the consumer a *possibility for change*. Without a possibility for change, there is no purpose in seeing a social worker, nor for that matter, in being a social worker. If life is but an inevitable series of circumstances over which the consumer has no control, the social worker can only seal ultimate doom. Social workers must *believe* a person can make choices in the world; they must *believe* that the world has a *potential* for changing. A predetermined world where all consumers are simply acting out assigned roles is an impotent world. The worker must sincerely believe in the potential of people and of the environment to change. For it is only this belief that will allow the worker to offer the consumer a "climate of possible change."

If the worker believes that the capitalistic system is immutable and not subject to human intervention, he or she has no "climate of hope" to offer the consumer who is a victim of economic discrimination. If the social worker feels, however, that a consumer can be helped to use the economic system to his or her own advantage, the worker can offer the consumer a climate of possible change.

If a social worker feels that loneliness is an essential reality of life, he or she can offer no climate of possible change to the consumer who is tormented by loneliness.

The climate of possible change must be based on the world as it is, not as it "could" be, on reality, not on romance and fantasy. To help the consumer to recognize potential choices for change, and ultimately to make those changes, the social worker must recognize the world as it is and the realistic potential for change within it.

For the beginning social worker, an understanding of change and potential change must be scaled down from magical fantasies of dramatic change to the actual changes in daily living that all too often are quite small, seemingly insignificant, often barely perceived. For example, the benefits of work with children may not be noted until adulthood. Social work is often pedestrian, sometimes minute, perhaps mundane. The changes are most frequently not monumental. But even the smallest change is vital when dealing with the human condition.

Beyond empathy and acceptance of the consumer as a human

being, the worker must offer the possibility of altering the condition that prompted the consumer to seek his help. When the reality itself cannot be changed, a change in the perception of the reality is essential.

A social worker in the Department of Social Services may alter a family's reality by providing the food, shelter, or medical assistance required. A social worker may alter a condition of loneliness by helping an older person become involved in a senior citizens club. A social worker may refer a couple wishing to adopt a child to the proper agency. A consumer addicted to drugs may be admitted to a system where help is given to relieve the addiction. Such circumstantial changes are easily identified. Here the social worker offers a "climate of possible change," almost reflexively, because resources are available to cope with problems of this nature. Society has recognized its obligations to its citizenry and has provided the resources for meeting such needs. Here the social worker is, essentially, bringing the person to the resources. (Although often much more difficult than suggested here, helping the person to the resource has always been an essential task of the social worker.)

But what climate of possible change can the social worker offer in those situations where the reality is inexorable? Where the disease, for example, is progressive and fatal; where death is imminent; where the limb has been severed from the body; where the sight is gone; where separation and loss have actually occurred and the bereaved survivor is inconsolable? In short, what climate of possible change can the social worker offer when the reality is inevitable and cannot be altered?

At the very least, the social worker must reflect the world as it is, warts and all. The perpetuation of myths, even benign myths, does not lie within the confines of professional help. As the ultimate arbiters of reality, social workers must shun a romantic view of the world and deal exclusively with realities.

Social workers, of course, deal with romance and fantasy as part of the human condition, but the distinction between the real and the unreal must always be observed.

It is extremely tempting to the beginning worker to reassure a consumer inappropriately, to say that everything will be all right, to attempt to stop the pain by denying it. It is tempting to reassure a child that life will be "wonderful" in the new foster home. It is difficult to tell the child that the situation may well be painful, but the job of the social worker is to help the child and the foster parents deal with the actuality of the situation and to offer a climate of possible change within the realities of the world.

The best a social worker can say to a couple who are having marital difficulties is that they are at a place "where we can examine the problems in your marriage together." There are no guarantees. Predictions of things to come remain the province of the psychic. Social workers who reassure inappropriately usually do it to satisfy their own needs to be liked and respected by the consumer, to control the life of the consumer, and to play "good person" and "supreme being." Naturally, when the needs being served are those of the worker, the needs of the consumer are no longer being met.

Inappropriate reassurance is a clear and persistent danger. There has not been a social worker yet who has not, in some manner, fallen prey to it. Reassuring inappropriately is an easy solution. In addition to meeting only the worker's own needs, false reassurance actually inhibits a meaningful transaction between the social worker and the consumer. To the consumer, inappropriate reassurance means that his or her problems are so great and so terrible that not even the social worker can cope with them. Inappropriate reassurance imprisons people in their own fantasies; it infantilizes them.

False reassurance also occurs, often more subtly, in the ongoing practice of social work, where it is as potentially disastrous as in the beginning. Only experience and good supervision can avoid the pitfall.

Although there is no escape from reality, the worker can nevertheless offer a climate of possible change, not a change in the reality itself but a change in the perception of the reality. The loss of a limb is real, but the consumer is alive and can exploit being alive to the maximum possible extent. The worker can help the consumer deal with his loss and express his intense feelings of deprivation. At the appropriate time, the worker can help the consumer integrate the pain and the loss and then move on with the process of living. The worker can help the consumer obtain and learn to use an artificial limb and rearrange his life-style to deal with his reduced physical capacity. The family, too, needs help in adjusting to the consumer's new situation. When the consumer with the artificial leg grabs the worker around the waist to dance a jig, it is not the reality that has changed but the consumer's perception of the reality.

The child whose parents were killed in an automobile accident must move into an adoptive home. She must be helped to deal with the fears, frights, disappointments, angers, the feelings of loss and deprivation, grief and mourning. "Don't worry, everything will be all right" won't do. The child must be allowed time to grieve, time to accept. She must be reassured that problems in adjusting to the new family situation can be worked out. And one day when she calls out to her new father and says, "Hey, John, let's take a bike ride," she will demonstrate that although the reality hasn't changed, her perception of it has.

With someone facing death, the social worker can help by just being there and allowing the consumer to express his fears. Once the terror that death holds is examined, a consumer is often able to accept it more easily and is thus released to continue living to the fullest extent possible for as long as possible.

These are extreme examples but they serve to illustrate the offer of a climate of possible change even under the most adverse situations. By working with and through feelings, a skilled and understanding social worker can help consumers arrive at new perspectives.

What Being a Consumer Means. A person who requests a change in his or her life becomes a consumer when an agreement, an informal contract, is reached between a social worker and the person to work together to make the desired change. The same definition applies to the person for whom society demands a change.

Change is defined in its broadest sense, from altering material or social circumstance to getting rid of a feeling, for example, or adding a new idea, an insight. Change, consequently, can occur in the physical and/or internal environment. The collaboration of the social worker and the consumer is based upon the mutual acceptance of change, whether it be in income, employment, living arrangements, recreational facilities, feelings and attitudes, communications, and so on.

The social worker is faced, from time to time, with requests for change that are patently impossible or even undesirable. A consumer with a prosthetic leg may want his own leg back, for example. Still, change is a possible goal. Perhaps the consumer's feelings about the leg can be changed. Help in accepting the loss of his leg or in developing more control in the use of the prosthetic leg may relieve the problem.

Mutuality. Work between a social worker and a consumer is a *mutual* endeavor. The concept of mutuality implies an agreement about the need for change and the assignment of respective tasks to both the social worker and the consumer to accomplish the desired change.

With the involuntary consumer, the mutuality is harder to come by. In a prison situation, for example, the consumer's participation may be minimal, because the prisoner has no personal desire for change and is participating only to avoid undesirable consequences. Thus, the prisoner "agrees" to "see" the social worker. Although reluctant and hostile, the prisoner has allowed a certain mutuality to be achieved. Because the prisoner's commitment to the contract is only to "see" the social worker, the burden of identifying the area to be changed and working toward it lies with the social worker, whose task is to involve the prisoner, to help him to assume a larger share in the proceedings. A glowering, nonverbal prisoner might be reached, for example, if the social worker were to simply verbalize his anger to him. Many techniques are available to help the social worker break through such walls with the end result being a greater commitment from the consumer to mutual work on the needed changes. Failure, however, is not uncommon, and the social worker must often settle for only the physical presence of the consumer.

Wearing the Consumer's Shoes. A worker's ability to identify with the consumer is essential. When one puts oneself in the consumer's shoes, one is better able to sense what the consumer is experiencing. Although this can never be absolute, it can be approximated. For example, how does an ad agency executive who has recently lost his lucrative job feel as he applies at the Department of Social Services for public assistance? Embarrassed? Shy? Angry? How would a consumer who is reapplying for public assistance after spending years in a mental hospital feel? A seasonal worker who must reapply for assistance when the season ends? Based on the nature of the agency and the preliminary information available, a social worker should be able to anticipate the general feelings to expect.

The feelings of parents applying to an agency to adopt a child would not be expected to be angry or indifferent but more anxious and concerned. A child going into a new foster home—fear, anxiety.

Although generalizations can be helpful, it must also be recognized that people react differently to similar situations. Embarrassed, one person might react by stuttering, blushing, or withdrawing. Another person, equally embarrassed, might react with bluff and hostility to cover the embarrassment. How consumers deal with their feelings in their initial approach to an agency frequently suggests how they react to other life situations. If a consumer does not react as normally expected, the social worker must determine why or reevaluate his or her own notions about the reaction to be expected.

Experience in an agency quickly gives a social worker some sense of the reaction to be expected from potential consumers. Predictions of initial reactions are based on the worker's knowledge of the nature of the agency's services, the intake record, which allows a gross assessment of the consumer's situation and the worker's own feelings: How would the *worker* feel if he or she were applying to this agency service?

To fully understand the consumer's emotional configuration, the worker must not only recognize a "frightened" consumer but also relate to the feeling. What happened "inside" the worker the last time he was frightened? His stomach curled up in a ball, he felt frozen, his mouth was dry. When workers can recall their own emotional responses in some detail, they are better able to understand what the consumer is "really" going through.

This exercise in the development of empathy helps the worker to relate more quickly to the consumer—to understand the consumer better, to be able to move toward the consumer with sensitivity. The worker does not anticipate a consumer's reaction to demonstrate one-upmanship but rather to facilitate an understanding on first contact.

Such pre-encounter work, of course, is only an aid. The reality of the experience itself takes precedence over the anticipation of the experience. If the worker's anticipations do not approximate reality, the new realities must be used to form new anticipations. The ongoing work proceeds in much the same way. Although it is often tempting to force facts to fit the theory, to help a consumer the theories must fit the facts.

The giver-receiver relationship often puts a distance between the social worker and the consumer. At times a social worker may want to maintain that distance, known as the *professional distance,* for a desired end. More often, however, the social worker attempts to establish a relationship of mutuality with ascribed roles for both partners in the endeavor.

During this pre-encounter phase workers can also draw on the experience of their suprevisors to assist them in preparing for the initial meeting with the consumer.

Role Playing. Role playing—the acting out of roles by the worker—is a technique often used in various phases of work to prepare the worker for new situations, to re-create consumer experiences, to reinforce work that has gone well, and to allow a worker to rethink a situation that has stymied progress.

In preparing for the pre-encounter phase a social worker acts out the part of either the worker or the consumer. As the former, the worker searches for appropriate ways to reach toward the consumer; as the consumer, the worker develops additional sensitivity to allow him to empathize with the consumer's feelings. Comments from objective observers to this enactment can add a dimension that is not available to the ''actors.''

For example, a new social worker, new to the field and new

to the agency, is preparing to meet a prospective consumer for the first time. The worker decides to play the role of the social worker and his supervisor, perhaps, the role of the consumer. After reading the intake material, the worker has a fairly accurate idea about what type of consumer to expect. An anticipation of the encounter can then be enacted.

As the "social worker," the worker greets the "consumer" for the first time. Going through the greetings and introductory remarks is an excellent learning experience. How does the worker say hello? What are the effects of the worker's initial comments on a potential consumer? What does he say after he says hello? The initial greeting is quite significant; it sets the tone for subsequent work. Good initial contact can speed up involvement considerably and poor initiation can retard it. The "consumer" responds, and from his reactions the newer worker gets a sense of how a real consumer might react to his overtures. After a piece of interaction, the enactment stops, the greeting, for example, and the work is reviewed. When both participants are involved in their roles, it is best that they stay in character, the "consumer" particularly. Feelings and reactions from both the "social worker" and the "consumer" are examined, interviewing techniques discussed, and new approaches identified. To correct some aspect of the greeting, the scene can be repeated, or the interview can move on. The enactment is interrupted when a strong response from one of the participants occurs. The discussion that follows is a unique learning experience, and one of the few instances when a worker can get a direct "consumer" response at no cost to a real situation. After playing the "worker" for awhile, the new worker should switch roles and become the "consumer." In this role the new social worker may experience how the consumer will react to the stress of the encounter, how it feels to get a "tough" question, what it means to be supported or not really listened to, and so on.

Role playing allows the repetition of material in those areas where the worker is having the most difficulty. It allows experimentation with various questions and responses and the working through of alternate responses. At the very least, role playing allows workers to develop a sense of ease with the various situations they will meet.

The tendency to respond with stereotyped reactions to specific situations is quickly identified and eliminated from the procedure. The purpose of role playing is to develop an objective spontaneity within a professional framework.

After the worker gets over the initial hesitancy of revealing his practice to someone else, his sense of role playing improves. When a group of new workers engages in role playing, they quickly learn that anxiety reactions, particularly in initial contacts, are not really unique, but rather universal reactions experienced by all new workers. That problems are not unique is not only a good thing to learn but also a good reassurance to have, particularly for new workers who often feel quite relieved when they see that they are not alone.

Role-playing enactments can be set up for all anticipated situations. How, for example, does a worker react to a hostile or resistant consumer? Having experienced the impact of an angry or threatening remark in the "safe" situation offered by role playing, the worker can avoid not only the sense of pain or outrage that an actual attack normally produces but also the development of a situation that might threaten the progress of an ongoing work relationship. The exploration of such a situation beforehand allows a worker a preview of the experience that may help him to maintain his objectivity when the actual situation occurs in practice.

The greater the experience gained in role playing, the more relaxed and natural the worker can be in professional encounters and freer, too, to discuss technique issues that arise in practice.

Role playing is limited by the fact that it can be only a representation of a previously experienced similar or anticipated situation. Actual practice reveals dimensions of reactions only vaguely suspected and not always anticipated. The real situation contains so many variables that only probabilities are identified, whereas possibilities are infinite. The momentum too of a real life work situation—the pacing, the timing, the continuity—is different from the simulation. Role playing has the unique advantage, however, in allowing the development of technique and learning beyond the individual characteristics of a particular case situation. Specific learning becomes incorporated into generalized practice procedure.

HELPING PEOPLE TO HELP THEMSELVES

"Helping people to help themselves" reflects a *process* of working with others to help them develop the resources that will allow them to not only improve their life-style but also become self-sufficient.

In the process of working through the consumer's problems to reach this goal, all the skills of the social worker are called into play—to supplement deficiencies, fill in informational gaps, provide services or direction to other services, educate, develop insight, and so on. "Helping people to help themselves" does not imply that the consumer is directed by the social worker along some predetermined pathway or even that the social worker knows what is good for the consumer. But it does imply a condition that allows consumers to become self-propelled, that is, a freedom to develop life-styles that reflect their own personal strengths, attitudes, and values.

The job of the social worker is completed, the goal is achieved, when the consumer no longer needs him or her—in effect, the business of social work is to put itself out of business.

People can most often help themselves when they understand the viable possibilities that exist to resolve a particular problem and are able to make a meaningful choice. It is the job of the social worker to provide the ambience where such understanding can occur. In working with a delinquent boy, for example, the social worker's goal is to provide a "choice" for the youngster to make, the suggestion being that new clothes can be obtained by stealing—or by buying. By developing a relationship with the boy and his family, the social worker seeks to help the youngster find a less punitive and more rewarding solution. Even institutionalization introduces an alternate life system, one that allows some opportunity for decision making. The introduction of "choice" involves a rethinking of the sole method of goal attainment (I want a car, I steal a car, I will go to jail) and the introduction of an alternate method of attaining the same goal (I want a car, I will work and save money to buy a car, I will not go to jail). This is but one of a number of possible alternatives.

Another way to introduce meaningful choices is to allow consumers to understand the psychological reasons behind their actions. For example, by helping the young car thief understand *why* he wants to steal a car (because I feel that I am not loved), what emotional needs stealing represents, and how stealing is connected to other aspects of his functioning, the social worker allows the youngster to choose alternate ways.

In working with the mentally ill, the social worker attempts to free the consumer from the neurotic manifestations that bind decision making. Through insight, the expression of feelings, support of the ego, alleviation of super-ego control, and reality identification, the consumer is freed to enjoy greater personal growth and to exercise more choice in life.

Poverty inhibits the decision-making process. The need to survive takes precedence over the luxury of decision making. People living in poverty, for example, have little choice over the handling of their welfare money—pay the rent or be evicted, buy food or starve. The choice is moot, the issue, major. As one moves up the economic ladder, choices obviously become wider.

Social work may be characterized as overcoming resistance to choices. For one consumer, information itself may provide a choice. Choices are limited by the knowledge at the consumer's disposal. When an adolescent girl, for example, is informed about birth-control measures, she is better able to make more realistic decisions about her sex life. Basic information about sexual practices, contraception, abortion procedures, adoption and foster care services, family planning, and so on can help a consumer to more fruitfully assess reality and consequently make more appropriate choices.

The family itself functions as either a choice inhibitor or a choice extender. Contemporary values versus traditional values often create conflicts within the family structure. Social work on the family level helps the family members recognize each other's needs on a more realistic basis, thus permitting greater, or at least more clarified, options.

In some situations choice is limited by an environmental situation. The task of the social worker is to identify the environmental limitation and attempt to alleviate it. Senior citizens, for example, in a community without a senior citizen center are limited. They do not have the choice of participating in a center's activities or remaining at home.

Choice, however, is not always available to all consumers. For some consumers—the very young, the very old, the physically and mentally ill—the social worker must provide a more structured, more directive service. A five-year-old child, for example, is not capable of deciding whether or not she needs a foster home or even which foster parents would be best for her.

The principle remains, however, and although the child cannot be allowed the above choice, she can be allowed to decide which dress to wear. To have her own domain recognized when catastrophic events seem to have rendered her helpless, is an important first step.

Knowing how and when and how much to encourage and support consumers in making their own decisions and when to take a more directive or controlling position is the applied art of social work. The passive social worker who cannot intervene in the life of the consumer permits the consumer to fail too often. Alternatively, the directive social worker who makes most of the decisions for the consumer creates additional dependency and infantilizes the consumer. In addition to denying the consumer the opportunity to choose, the situation also denies the consumer a sense of both success and failure that is uniquely his own.

Throughout the practice of social work, even in areas where social control is paramount, the concept of helping people to help themselves remains valid. When a consumer is deprived of physical freedom, when children are removed from their parents to protect the children, the social worker can still help these consumers make decisions in those areas where decision making is still possible. The prisoner, for example, can be helped to use his time in a more constructive way, and the parents can be helped to prepare themselves for the eventual return of their children. Although restricted by circumstances or by law, choice in some areas is aways available.

To help consumers assume more control over their own lives by making them more aware of what options are available and helping them to remove the barriers that prevent the exercise of those options, the social worker should

- be aware of the consumer's strengths and limitations.
- provide information about the services that are available, where

such services are located, and what the requirements for service are. (Choice is often limited simply because consumers are uninformed about available services.)

- help the consumer work through the self-erected personal barriers that serve to limit choice. (This difficult task requires social workers to involve themselves intensely with the emotional and value concepts of another person. Such workers generally realize that their own values are the result of choices.)
- help the consumer, when appropriate, to make use of other resources—family, friends, community.
- help only in the areas where help is needed and work toward the goal of independence for the consumer.

Groups too need to learn to help themselves. In group work, the social worker, as leader, constantly strives toward this end in addition to working with individual members. The social worker helps the group to accomplish its contracted tasks, to deal with the barriers to completion, to assume new directions in the pursuit of its goals, to be aware of other courses of action. The worker emphasizes and works toward increased group autonomy.

In a group situation the tendency of the social worker is to do more rather than less. The ill-defined nature of professional "help" and the lack of objective completion criteria tend to lend an air of insecurity about the helping process itself. Insecurity, in turn, leads to overkill, under the mistaken impression that *doing* more means *helping* more. In the area of social work, as in the environmental context, less is often more.

Doing for consumers what they can do for themselves promotes a concept of consumer inadequacy. Making mistakes is part of living and growing and the social worker must help consumers in appropriate situations to make their own mistakes, to learn from them, and to be responsible for them. In all fairness, however, if it is a question of doing too much or too little for a consumer, it is usually best to do too much.

The needs of the consumer determine the activity of the social worker. The amount of help given is determined by an assessment of the strengths and limitations of the consumer. An absolutely helpless consumer needs absolute help. But even in a circumstance of "absolute" helplessness, the consumer's responsibility for his or her own life should be allowed to increase and the social worker's responsibility to decrease.

FIVE

UNDERSTANDING OTHERS– COMMUNICATION

Communication is accomplished by verbal and nonverbal mechanisms that both promote and disguise understanding. The signals people use are often complex, contradictory, and, at times, even poorly understood by the communicator. Social workers, of course, must recognize and interpret the consumer's signals as well as their own. Are both parties signaling to each other what they *really* mean?

VERBAL COMMUNICATION

As a most significant tool for man, words have allowed him a means of communicating ideas and facts, thoughts and feelings. Like other tools, however, words can serve other purposes as well. Words can be used to manipulate, to identify or camouflage the true state of affairs, to restructure reality, to provide deception. To a large extent, how a word is used is dependent upon the person using it. Words can be used almost at will to suit any particular need or desire, and they often fail even when there is no intention to disguise. However, because of this flexibility and the socially determined role of words, they often are not the most accurate indicators of the facts. For example, a child with jam on his hands turns his face away in shame as he mumbles that he has *not* been eating between meals; a woman with tear-stained cheeks says, "No, no, everything is fine"; a man, fists at the ready, glares angrily at the social worker while *saying* through clenched teeth how much he likes to come to the sessions.

At times a person may deliberately camouflage his actions to consciously protect his real meanings from becoming known. In applying for a job, for example, a person may disguise his real feelings of insecurity and concern about whether he can do the job or not with an aggressive positiveness and bold brashness.

Obviously, words themselves are not always reliable. The spoken word must be verified, by other perceptions, that is, hand gestures, body movements, and tone of voice. And if verification belies the words, then the verification takes precedence. That "actions speak louder than words" is not to be forgotten. The shrug of a shoulder is often more devastating than paragraphs of audible sound.

VERBAL COMMUNICATION IN SOCIAL WORK

Words, of course, are a basic tool in the interaction between a social worker and a consumer. But it is only when the words, the tone of voice, the gestures, the feelings, and the history and the present reality come together and mesh that it can be reasonably assumed that the consumer has communicated the truth of the matter. A discrepancy in any of these factors suggests that the consumer is not yet ready to divulge, or accept, the real situation.

In assessing the reality of, but not judging, the activities of others, it must be recognized that all people have the need, and the right, to dissemble, to *not* be completely open, to disguise and protect themselves from others. Words allow this protection and may be so appropriately used. Thus, a discrepancy between a word and an action is not cause for confrontation. Rather, the social worker should tuck the observation away, to be used or not at some other time, depending on the situation.

Insofar as verbalizations represent controllable expressions, they are recognized as being important. It is a consumer's fundamental right to project himself in a particular manner; it is the social worker's obligation to respect that right. The issue represented here is self-determination. Verbal communications permit whatever degree of privacy or accuracy that is chosen. Until such time as the contract between the consumer and the social worker deems otherwise, the right to choose one's words must be respected.

The social worker has a need to "know" the consumer in order to help. To better understand a consumer, a social worker observes nonverbal cues, attempts to recognize what lies behind the words, and interprets silences.

Words can be transformed by social workers into understandings that help identify more clearly the "world" of the consumer—where he comes from, what he is struggling with, how he sees his problems. When the consumer's world is identified, his reaction to that world can be better understood. With this information, the social worker and the consumer can work together to resolve the situation.

Words provoke various reactions in human beings. Verbal abuse often provokes anger or withdrawal; lying provokes resentment or chagrin. In the unique world of social work, however, the common "human" response is not allowed; the social worker must react in a controlled manner. When a consumer "lies," for example, the social worker suspends the usual response and asks instead: "What does this activity mean?" The act of "lying" itself is a communication from the consumer to the worker. What is that communication? Is the consumer saying that he doesn't trust the social worker or the agency? . . . that he is too frightened to tell the truth? . . . that he is unable to not continually distort the world? . . . that the situation is too sensitive and difficult for him to deal with? From such a chain of questions the social worker comes to an understanding of what the "lie" means. Because it is being used to serve a purpose, lying by a consumer is neither good nor bad from a worker's point of view. Like other activities, it is a piece of behavior that is only to be understood.

Beginning social workers are often upset when a consumer lies to them. "Here am I trying to help—and he lied to me!" The insult is, at times, too much to bear. The question is, "Whose needs are being served here?" The answer is obvious. The consumer has failed to respond to the social worker's need to see himself as "someone to be trusted." But the consumer is not there to help the social worker. In learning how to depersonalize emotionally charged material, the worker also learns how to put the issue back where it belongs. Not "he is hurting me" but "why does he feel it is necessary to hurt me?" The social worker must place the problem in its proper perspective—on the needs of the consumer.

Verification of Verbalization. That behavior in isolation is least understood is particularly true with respect to verbal expressions. To appropriately assess verbal expressions, the worker must observe them in relation to behavior.

When an expensive automobile draws up at a public-assistance agency and a young man flicking a speck of dust from his Pierre Cardin suit steps out and announces that he is in need of food stamps, the incongruity of his appearance and his words might raise a questioning eyebrow.

The gross disparity between the behavioral cues—the suit, the limousine—and the verbal expression is obvious. When another young man appears at the public-assistance agency on foot, wearing old clothes, unshaven, and utters the same words, however, the response would be different. The behavioral cues match the verbal expression, a reality situation. In neither case, at this time, is there a rush to judgment; initial assessments are always subject to verification or change as information is developed.

Thus, as important as verbal expressions are, they are perhaps not always the best indicator of the real state of affairs. Nonverbal indicators—what a consumer *does* as opposed to what he *says*—are often closer to the mark.

Words—Facts. Words not in accordance with other information often signal that something is awry and indicate a need for further investigation. For example, last week a consumer said his father was dead. Today he reports he and his father had a beer last night. What is happening? Either the information is erroneous or the consumer is experiencing some difficulty—only further investigation will clarify.

In addition to observing such discrepancies, the social worker must be alert to what is being said and what is known or thought to be known in regard to each incident, no matter how small, for when combined, seemingly innocuous discrepancies may indicate more serious areas to be investigated.

Words—Affects. Verbal expressions, however, are not just flat sounds enunciated in a certain determined manner with certain agreed upon meanings. Verbal expressions are colored with ''feelings'' that spring up surrounded with emotion. Technically, the feeling tones surrounding expressions are known as *affects*. A social worker must ''tune'' in to this layer of verbal expression as well. What do the feeling tones beneath the words really signal? When the words are sad, yet the affect is joyous, some serious questions may be raised. Why don't the words match the feelings, what is being said here? Does the consumer mean what his words are saying—that he is sad? Or does he mean what his affect is communicating—that he is joyous? Affect, like other nonverbal communications, is often a more valid indicator of where a person really is than is his verbal expression of the situation.

Affect is a very strong communication device. To a social worker, affect is a "must" of awareness to be listened for in every situation. Consider: "I got a new job," the consumer says in a flat monotone with no discernible affect in his voice. What does he mean? Why isn't he excited? Doesn't he care? Doesn't he want the job? Is he depressed about the whole thing? Is that his way of communicating joy because any genuine signs of joy will antagonize the gods and they will take the job away from him? The real answer depends on other information, other cues and messages.

"I got a new job!" another consumer says excitedly, eyes sparkling, his hands gesturing exuberantly. What does this mean? Here the words and the affect are making the same signals, both communicating the same thing. Here, all other things being equal, the words and the affect can be interpreted to mean what they say.

"*I* got a new job!" another consumer says incredulously, his eyes saucers of disbelief, his palms upraised uncertainly. Does this mean, "Gee, I got this new job and I can't believe my good fortune—wasn't I lucky?" Or does it mean the reverse, "Who needs this new job? I didn't apply for the damn thing. They gave it to me when I wasn't looking and everybody knows that it is a funky assignment." Here again, only knowledge of the consumer, his history, his other behavioral characteristics will lead to the correct assessment.

"I got a . . . new . . . job," another consumer says hesitantly. Here the affect says, "I'm biting my nails with worry and I'm very nervous and I don't know whether or not I can really make it work." The words and the affect match.

The affect, the feeling tones that accompany the words, must be heard and understood. It is a strong indicator of what is really happening with a consumer, stronger than the words themselves. In each example above, the words communicated the same information; the affect, however, varied from instance to instance. Sooner or later, it is the affect that must be addressed.

Words—Silence. In a consumer/worker relationship silence is often as significant as verbal communication. Social workers, continually alert to "signals," are aware that a consumer's silence can signal a difficult area in the consumer's life. When listening to words, a social worker attempts, using his knowledge, the ancillary cues, and observation, to sift through the layers of words to understand the underlying meaning. As silence is a symbolic interpretation of a state of being, it too is a communication.

A social worker fears (or so he imagines) rejection by a consumer only a bit more than he fears silence in his work. When the education and professional ambience of the social worker are considered—a constant involvement with spoken and written words—difficulties in dealing with silence become more understandable. Dealing with words is the social worker's principal method of work. Consider a group situation in which ten silent people are staring at each other. When a consumer is "talking" at least something is being accomplished—the consumer and the worker are "doing something" together. Ten people sitting, staring, silent. The social worker asks himself: "What does this group mean by its silence?"

- Are they *afraid* to talk? (Reassurance about the worker/consumer relationship may hurdle this block.)
- Is the group uncertain about what it is supposed to do? (A redefinition of the purpose of the group may initiate discussion.)

- Is the group confused? (Additional explanation of the purpose of the group may resolve the confusion.)
- Is the group thinking deeply about the preceding discussion? (This kind of silence can be allowed; the group members need time to work out and absorb the insight.)
- Is the group angry with the leader? (The worker must identify the anger and work with the group members to help them recognize and deal with it.)
- Is the group thinking about other times and places? (A restatement of purpose may move them back to the issue.)
- Is the subject under discussion too difficult to deal with at this time? (The worker may move the group away from the difficult area or help the members to deal with it.)

The reason for the silence determines the next step. When the worker does not have a reasonable interpretation of the silence, the question can be directed to the group.

Silence, like words, must de listened to in order to be understood. Silences are messages, cues, indicators, signposts. When silence is understood for what it really is—communication—how to work with it becomes a matter of course.

THE ART OF LISTENING

Social workers themselves are the primary instruments through which they help others. Many of their professional techniques are common, everyday activities that other people do, as well, such as listening.

But listening to a professional social worker is not the simple act of *hearing* what another person is *saying*. It is rather an *understanding* of what the other person is *meaning*. Because meanings are often veiled in self-protective devices, the social worker knows that a person does not always mean what he says.

It is necessary for the social worker to understand the factors that create and influence the consumer and also to fathom where the consumer is and what he wants at any given point in time. Listening requires a sensitivity to nuances and as a conscious act allows the worker to decipher whatever protective language the consumer chooses to use.

At the same time, listening to words for the facts they convey is, of course, equally essential. In order for the social worker to concentrate on the facts the consumer is relating, he must set aside his own problems and attempt to "be with" the consumer. Unencumbered by his own interests and life situation, he can hear the informational aspects of the communication in as pure or unfiltered a manner as possible.

Beginning social workers, being so intent on unraveling the *meaning,* sometimes fail to recognize the factual content. They fall into the trap of understanding what a consumer is *meaning* but do not have the vaguest idea of what the consumer is saying.

What the consumer is "saying" is what the consumer "wants" the worker to hear. His spoken words are what he is permitting the worker to recognize about him—this is a "defense," the posture he presents, the announcement to the world of who and what he is. From this perspective, this fundamental "right" of the consumer must be respected and automatically acknowledged in the work situation. This is where the consumer "is" and the worker must be where the consumer "is" in order to help. But again, facts without meaning are worthless.

If the worker pays attention to only what is being said and not to the meaning of what is being said, he can often miss the communication. When disappointed by the action of a consumer, a new worker often complains: "But he said he *would* come next week, and he didn't!" As if words and meanings were the same!

In these situations, a review of the interview with the consumer may reveal the clues that convey the real meaning of the situation.

When a mildly ill child, grinning from ear to ear, says he will miss school, even a doting parent might observe the incongruity between what the child is saying and what he actually means. This sense of what is going on under the factual level of communication is experienced by everyone and, for the most part, little attention is paid to those underlying communications. It is only when the incongruity between what is being said and what is being expressed is striking that people react.

When factual content and emotional meanings are not congruent, people sense and react to the discrepancy with curiosity, incredulity, anger, or by simply denying the content. To hear the subtle incongruities as well as the blatant, the social worker must listen consciously and sensitively to the content and meaning simultaneously.

Below the factual and meaning levels there is another, the *latent* level, often unrecognized by the persons themselves, which is more primitive, more basic, and more representative of where the person is really at.

The feelings lodged on the latent level are only vaguely sensed; lurking on the fringes of consciousness, they are yet potent enough to be perceived as frightening. Alien and unacceptable, these feelings and thoughts are often totally banned from consciousness. On an even deeper level lie the thoughts, feelings, instincts, and drives that are always prohibited entry to the conscious level. Many mental health theoreticians and practitioners believe that this level, the unconscious, is the principal motivational force for all human activity.

When parts of the latent world intrude into the conscious world, they intrude because of their own need to be expressed. As a whole, in the varied nightmarish atmosphere of the latent level, the recognized realities of life no longer hold true, contradictions exist side by side, forbidden wishes and animalistic instincts prevail, unthinkable, erotic, murderous thoughts reign. That most people cannot or will not recognize this level is understandable. Although the trained professional, of course, recognizes the latent level, whether it is used in actual professional work can be determined only by the conditions and purposes of the worker/consumer contract.

Working with latent material is one method of offering help. At one time in the history of social work, it was *the* method of offering service; currently it is but one of several. Working with latent material is dependent on the nature and purpose of the agency, the nature of the consumer's difficulty, and the consumer's informed permission. Regardless of the validity of its use, its existence and its influence must be recognized by the social worker.

For the social worker to provide the most *effective* service possible, an understanding of the inner world of the consumer is vital. A consumer's right to privacy is not violated by the worker's knowledge of his latent world, for it is through this understanding that the consumer can be better served.

Theodor Reik referred to this search for latent meanings as "listening with the third ear," an apt and dramatic expression. The two ordinary, everyday ears hear the words for their simple content. But the "third ear," located inside the head somewhere, hears the meanings behind the words.

Listening for both the manifest and the latent content occurs simultaneously, once the necessary attention has been directed to it. Once again, what is really happening is the development of more and more sensitivity.

Good supervision is necessary to help the student and the beginning worker in the area of latent meanings. The objectivity of the supervisor helps the new worker learn how to screen out his subjective response to the latent messages and to become more selective and focused in his listening with the third ear.

"What does that really mean?" can stimulate the third ear. The worker becomes aware, for example, of the "feeling" tones beneath the words, of the emotional attachments and weights that are contained in the verbal flow, of the volume, the loudness or softness, of the words. Why are some words accented and bellowed forth, and others so soft and barely heard? Why is he talking so fast? Why so slowly? Why does he pause before the word "mother"? Why is he stuttering? The worker's third ear, like a radar screen, reads impulses, sorts them out, deciphers the code. Once the technique of listening with the third ear is developed, the questions and answers blend, the minuscule threads of content bind into ever larger strands, and the pattern, the texture, of the individual emerges.

Listening with the third ear is, of course, not merely auditory. It is a combination of sight, touch, and smell, as well. Through visual observation, through the shake of a hand, through the musty, dank smell of the tenement, meanings are conveyed to the third ear.

Social workers should also "listen" for another communication, the communication of their own feelings. Through experience gained in dealing with other people's feelings, the social worker can learn to permit his own feelings to "sense" when the consumer is not communicating something he should. When he is hiding something "wrong," when things are "better" or "worse" than they appear to be. Experienced social workers develop an intuitive feel about what is going on, perhaps derived from cues so subtle that the workers are unaware of their influence. The message is nevertheless communicated and the worker almost intuitively responds. This is a delicate procedure, the prerogative of only the most experienced professional, and must be substantiated as well by an objective observer before intervention can be undertaken. It is mentioned here only to illustrate the very complex nature of human interaction.

To extend "listening" to its final dimension requires the ability to listen not only to what is being communicated, but to what is *not* being communicated. Why is there no expression of pain where there is loss? Why is there no expression of joy when there is good fortune? The "why nots" are as significant as the "whys," perhaps even more so.

Listening! How workers listen determines their effectiveness.

WHAT THE WORKER'S WORDS MEAN TO THE CONSUMER

As verbal interaction is a two-way street, the social worker must be conscious of not only the consumer's statements and their underlying meaning but his own as well. As the words of the consumer are significant to the social worker, so the worker's words are significant to the consumer.

The initial encounters, "Yes, I want to help you"—"Tell me about your situation so that I can understand it better"—"I think that I could be of some help if you would . . ." are well-meant attempts to reach out to another person. But should a consumer respond favorably to a worker's words? Why should he trust them, any more than the worker "trusts" the words of the consumer. As the social worker is assessing the consumer, the consumer is assessing the social worker. The words of a social worker are not enough. Actions, too, can provide a validity to the words that, over time, may persuade a consumer to trust the social worker with the turmoil of his inner self. Although in the initial contact only the tentative beginnings of this mutual trust can be tendered, the initial perception of the worker by the consumer is, obviously, basic to the ongoing relationship.

Is the consumer comfortable? Did the worker offer him a chair? Is the worker listening patiently, devoting his full attention to what the consumer is communicating? Do the worker's questions indicate attention and interest? Were the worker's services offered with warmth and concern? It is only in a climate of trust that true communication with another person can flourish.

The social worker who is natural, who is himself, is able to communicate the concern and the interest necessary to persuade the consumer to reciprocate, whereas the social worker who pretends interest or concern or who is oversolicitous in the "role" of social worker tends, rather, to alienate the consumer.

NONVERBAL COMMUNICATION

To *tell* a child that he is loved is one thing. To put an arm around a child and hug him, another.

When words fail us—what then? To paraphrase the old saying, one gesture is sometimes worth a thousand words. The uplifted palm, the shoulder shrug, the single tear, the gleeful smile with which a child salutes his first step, the sense of joy that emanates from the whole body of the football hero as he jubilantly spikes the ball after scoring—the nonverbal messages of the human system of communication are, to the social worker, often more reliable guideposts to the inner person than the spoken word.

Observation—The Home Visit. In many agencies the social worker, as a matter of course, visits the consumer in his home. Now less frequent because of economic pressures, the home visit, when possible, is often a source of valuable information. The home itself, as a reflection of the consumer—his family, how they live, what is important to them, artifacts that indicate sociocultural attitudes—provides clues to the total person.

The home visit, made with the consumer's permission, is designed not to value-judge but to secure information in order to provide better service. The social worker is not concerned with whether a "clean" house is better than a "dirty" house, but a "dirty" house, like a "clean" house, suggests some possibilities about the people who live there.

A dirty, sparsely furnished home may reflect a sense of defeat, a surrender, a hopelessness about life. It may reflect poverty, it may reflect a disinterest in conventional standards, whereas the huge library of technical books on the dirty shelves may reflect the values of another culture.

Home visits may suggest to the social worker certain questions, questions that he may want to examine later in the office with the consumer or may simply store away with other information to complete the picture of the total consumer. When visiting a dirty home in an upper-class neighborhood, for example, the following questions might arise: Did a sudden change in the family's economic status produce this disparity between community standards and individual living standards? Is this an isolated family with no concern or contact with the outside world? Is this family from a different climate, a different culture from their neighbors? If so, do these differing standards cause difficulty for the family? Is this family deliberately defying community standards? If so, why? Are there other possibilities to account for the disparity? Questions of mental health? Education? Information? Religion?

Conversely, visiting a "normal" home that "fits" neighborhood standards can be just as provocative to the skilled social worker as a visit to a home that deviates dramatically from the norm. Such a home might suggest such questions as: Does this indicate that the family has made a good adjustment to the community or are they simply conforming to social pressures? Are they unable to make individual decisions?

By no means exhaustive, these questions serve only to illustrate the type of thinking the social worker engages in, in attempting to understand a new situation through the simple process of observation. The observation must be objective, but what may appear to be trivial, or commonplace, often provides the worker with significant clues.

Observation: The Person. The "professional" self of the worker takes over when the potential consumer is first seen. Before even a word is exchanged, the physical appearance of the consumer is being professionally assessed. Young or old? Man or woman? Black? White? Other? Tall? Short? Fat? Skinny? Such essential but commonplace information will be subsequently recorded as: "Mr. X is a medium sized, black man of about forty years of age . . ."

These items may be relevant or irrelevant, depending upon the agency, the neighborhood, the services being offered. If the neighborhood is "white," what are the consequences, if any, of a black person living there? If it is an ethnically mixed or a liberal neighborhood, being black would prove irrelevant and slip back into obscurity.

Is the consumer's age relevant? Is the fact that the consumer is a black male of forty years significant? The answer depends on the nature of the services of the agency.

At this point in the relationship, the facts are simply observed. The information may become pertinent at some later point, depending upon additional information, the nature of the problem to be addressed, and the working arrangement between the worker and the consumer. It is the learning and working experience that develops in the worker the ability to distinguish what is important from what is not important.

A beginning social worker might not question why a father came to ask about his child. But a supervisor might observe: "That's odd, usually the mother comes." Whether this observation is relevant or not depends, of course, on the situation. The point is simply that the observation was made and could be important.

A student working in a state psychiatric hospital for an entire semester neglected to report to his supervisor that one particular patient was grossly overweight, indeed, was elephantine in appearance. This information had neither been recorded nor discussed with the supervisor. The fact finally surfaced, however, like a bombshell, for it brought together a whole constellation of information that had previously been a shapeless unfathomable mass. The revelation provided a whole new perspective and allowed an adequate assessment of the patient. The student now understood why he had felt so uncomfortable with the patient, as though the patient never had enough of him, as though the patient wanted to suck him dry. The student was then able to understand the patient's need to *control,* through weight, others and the world. With this understanding, the student was better able to help the patient establish more control over his own life.

The student's initial evaluation of the weight factor as irrelevant was, of course, inaccurate. In this particular case, weight, over which human beings have some degree of control, was being used to project an "image." What is merely a fact to the lay observer becomes a *significant* fact to the trained eye. If read correctly, obesity can often indicate how the consumer really feels about himself. A frightened person trying to "protect" himself from a hostile world shrouds himself with protective fat. A consumer whose infantile oral needs were never fully satisfied attempts to rectify that lack. A ghetto resident who can only afford starches suffers the consequent obesity. A member of a cultural group that prizes weight as an attribute of physical beauty adds pounds daily. Weight, an easily observable fact, is often a significant clue in the attempt to understand another person.

Dress, too, is an obvious characteristic, which, to a trained social worker, can signal the state of a person's being. Clothes, after all, are chosen for a reason and often provide another non-verbal communication. Why is this consumer dressed this way? Why is this woman's dress torn and dirty, her stockings dragging about her ankles? Too poor to buy clothes? Too emotionally upset at the moment to care? Not her usual appearance, was she in an auto accident? A poor self-image allows her to degrade herself? Psychotic, not aware of the world? In defiance of social conventions?

Another client, a young man dressed in a clean, well-pressed suit, white shirt and tie, polished shoes—is he in harmony with himself and his surroundings? Is he coming apart at the seams but compelled to present an in-command image? Is he trying to convey success, firmness, that he is secure in who he is and what he is doing? Is his appearance a defense against allowing a hostile world to see him as he really is?

Dress, like other aspects of a person, communicates. At this point questions not answers are material. What is the consumer trying to communicate through his or her clothing? The questions, once raised, can be resolved during the course of the relationship. It should be noted that these are not value questions, not "good" or "bad." Social workers forgo that luxury in a professional situation. "Do we like it?" is replaced by "What does it mean?"

Isolated verbal and nonverbal communications are of little value. It is only when such characteristics are combined with other communications that they begin to assume significance: a well-dressed consumer in a slum neighborhood; a tattered and torn consumer on Park Avenue; a seventy-year-old in teeny-bopper attire.

Communication is a complex phenomenon. To break it down into such discrete units is quite artificial but perhaps necessary to allow the recognition that in a series of individual communications certain patterns begin to emerge to delineate a dynamic whole.

Observation: The Face and the Body. Facial expressions often convey meaningful communications. The alert social worker observes their significance and integrates their meanings into the ongoing work. When the consumer is not conscious of his facial expression, it is more apt to reflect his real feelings, and that, of course, is what the social worker is looking for—what the person is really experiencing. Is the smiling consumer happy or simply obeying a social custom? Regardless of the image the consumer tries to present, he cannot be aware of every nuance that he might be projecting. And sometimes, of course, the consumer cannot even control his body. His autonomic nervous system may cause his knee to jerk in an anxious situation; and perspiring hands are not uncommon when meeting a new employer. When a person feels good—he is with the world and the world is with him—he stands straighter and walks taller. Conversely, if he experiences failure or is anxious or depressed, his shoulders sag, and he almost seems to creep into himself.

In assessing communication, particularly nonverbal communication, a major consideration is the *appropriateness* of the behavior—does it "fit" the situation. For example, trembling, hesitancy, tentativeness, all indicative of anxiety, would be expected from a consumer seeking help with a difficult emotional problem. When the behavior is in contrast to the reality of the problem or situation, however—a weeping consumer in a humorous situation—the social worker must ask, "What world is *this* consumer reacting to at *this* time?'' The consumer may be caught up in a personal situation of sadness and be unable to relate to humor, or perhaps the humor triggered a painful personal association that led to tears. Inappropriate behavior may result from a cultural variant not yet understood by the worker. Or the consumer might actually be psychotic, literally existing in another world. Nonverbal behavior is, obviously, an extremely important indicator of where a person really is.

Communication, then, is a two-way street. There will be traffic jams and an accident or two, perhaps, and now and then a detour, but the rules of the road will sustain the travelers to their destination.

SIX

THE
INTERACTION

All social work interactions can be divided into four major phases.

1. *The pre-encounter,* in which the intake procedure is completed and the worker interviews, when necessary, the consumer's family, community representatives, and so on, to prepare the necessary background on the case.
2. *The encounter,* in which the worker meets the consumer for the first time and works out a contract with the consumer.
3. *The ongoing interaction,* in which the worker and consumer actually work through the consumer's problem and all its ramifications.
4. *Termination,* in which the contract is terminated and the consumer is separated from the worker following an evaluation of the experience.

THE PRE-ENCOUNTER

Success or failure is often determined by pre-encounter efforts. Such efforts may even determine whether or not a service is accepted by the consumer in the first place. Workers, for example, who are uninformed about the operations and services of their own agency do little to inspire confidence in potential consumers.

The Intake Process

The intake process is the procedure that allows the consumer to use the services offered. Through the intake, or access, process, the nature of the service is defined for the consumer. At the same time, the intake process allows the agency to regulate its service flow as well as to define the types of problems it chooses to deal with. Through the intake process some consumers are accepted, others rejected, and still others are referred to other agencies. The consumer, too, may choose to accept or to reject services. Generally, the intake process allows an agency to maintain its organizational boundaries, which, in turn, justify its existence and define its purposes to the community.

Intake policies vary from agency to agency, reflecting the specific requirements of each particular service delivery system. In some agencies the intake procedure is quite elaborate, requiring a time-consuming, intricate process of negotiation before mutual agreement for service is reached. Considerable effort is required on the consumer's part, for along with factual information he must share with the agency his feelings and attitudes. Acceptance may occur only after the agency staff—social worker, psychologist, psychiatrist—has had an opportunity to meet and to discuss the individual circumstances. Acceptance, however, does not necessarily mean that service is immediately forthcoming; frequently, the consumer is put on a waiting list until services are available.

At the other end of the intake scale are systems that offer service instantly. Eligibility is established by walking through the door. In adolescent walk-in systems one's name is frequently not even required.

And beyond the consumer-initiated encounter there is the outreach program, in which the service seeks out the consumer, rather than the consumer the service.

The closer one moves into the community, the less formalized and structured the intake procedures. Access to service has always been considered a significant component of service delivery, for complicated forms, red tape, and alien procedures often effectively deter from the service those who need the service the most.

Community service groups, self-help organizations, and services dealing with more immediate and urgent social problems—store-front, crisis-oriented services that deal with potential suicides, runaways, and addicts—often forgo the formal application mechanisms usually employed.

Consumers often view intake procedures as barriers to service rather than as supports for service. The highly structured and formal intake procedure of the Department of Social Services, for example, requires that services be granted not by expression of need but by documentation of need. Reflecting a history of both a reluctance to provide and a suspicion of need, the Department of Social Services is to many of those in need a symbol of denial rather than of acceptance.

A successful service delivery system reflects the values and concerns of the community. An awareness of the sociocultural differences and of the variety of life-styles in the community is a minimum requirement, especially so when an agency composed of middle-class professionals is serving a lower-class neighborhood. The inability to surmount sociocultural differences is sometimes so severe that the program is not viable. An awareness of and respect for differing views is even more significant in anticipating and preventing emergency needs and crises. The access to and delivery of services are more effective when the life-styles of the consumers take precedence over needs and values of agency administration.

Consider, for example, a ritualized intake process—interviews, screenings, applications, psychological testing, psychiatric consulting, social work family assessment—in relation to a habitual drug user seeking help to break his addiction. He would be long gone before the first application was completed. However, a bank manager seeking help with marital difficulties would have serious questions as to what was going on if he did *not* receive a full assessment procedure. And similarly, to allow a couple to adopt a child simply because they walked through an agency doorway and requested a child would hardly be professional.

The intake process establishes the initial atmosphere of the agency to the prospective consumer. It sets a tone as to what can be expected from the agency. A brusque, unfeeling series of questions thrown at the new consumer does not invite participation, trust, or the expectation of helpful things to come. A consumer who manages to survive a hostile intake experience tends to be an angry and hostile client. Consequently, before the real problems can be dealt with the social worker has to resolve the resistances created by an insensitive introduction to the agency. Conversely, a sensitive and concerned intake worker can facilitate the future relationship of the consumer and the social worker by recognizing the consumer as a person and treating his concerns as serious matters. The consumer may even survive the intake procedure with some expectation that help is on the way.

Unfortunately, some agencies consider the intake process an irksome chore and assign the task to the least experienced worker. A "good" intake can be of enormous help to both the consumer and the social worker. It is the wise agency that assigns such responsibility to the most rather than the least experienced worker.

The "Face Sheet." Although the intake process varies from agency to agency, the following basic steps are generally required.

First the intake worker with the help of the consumer completes a "face sheet," a printed form that is standard for all cases. It contains such information as name, address, age, ethnic background, names of family members, interested relatives, and the consumer's reason for seeking help, which is called the presenting problem. Information relative to the specific function of the agency is included. For example, medical references are included in a hospital face sheet; job information in a welfare face sheet, and a face sheet for an abortion center may not require a name. From a practical point of view, a face sheet is an important document. For the lack of an apartment number many hours are lost in futile wanderings through tenements. Incorrect, out-of-date, or missing phone numbers, as well as misspelled names, cause endless frustration.

A "good" intake also marshals the existing details, sorts out important information, and presents a general statement about the consumer and his need for service. It also includes a description of the prospective consumer, his appearance and attitude. A perceptive intake worker can provide important information to the social worker who will eventually be working with the consumer. The intake procedure marks the beginning of the study process.

The sensitive intake worker also provides the prospective consumer with information about the service, bearing in mind that the initial atmosphere is pertinent to the future work that may occur. If the agency is not appropriate for the consumer's needs, the intake worker refers the consumer elsewhere with the same sensitivity that would be exercised if the consumer were to remain.

The Presenting Problem. As identified by the intake worker, the presenting problem is the reason, as "the client sees it," for seeking help. The presenting problem may or may not be the *real* reason the consumer came for assistance.

A stooped, somewhat disheveled elderly woman appears in the doorway of a senior citizens center. Seeming a little lost and confused, she says that she is not sure that the amount of her social security check is correct. Could the worker check it for her? During the conversation, the worker notices that the older woman is glancing around the center, observing the activities. The worker begins to sense that the woman has come to the agency for more than social security verification. When the worker concludes the discussion about the check, he suggests that she tour the center and introduces her to some of the members. He explains how the center works and offers her the opportunity to use its facilities. Yes, she would like that very much. Her husband died recently and she hasn't been able to get out much. She has only a few friends and would be interested in the program.

In this example, the presenting problem is the information the woman wanted about social security, which will, of course, be answered as soon as possible. But it was soon apparent to the social worker that perhaps another more significant reason had prompted her to seek out the agency. Observing the woman's loneliness and her curiosity about the center, the worker acted on this observation. Subsequent work with this woman may investigate the "real" problem—a need for friendship and social involvement.

Although the presenting problem may be the *real* problem, it often happens that the consumer is uncomfortable with the symptoms of the problem but not truly aware of the *real* problem. Or the consumer may be aware of the real problem but unable, for various reasons, to express it immediately. The woman at the senior citizens center, for example, found it acceptable to seek out information regarding her social security check, but she was not ready to admit that she was lonely and needed companionship. To her, loneliness may reflect a certain lack on her part, a sense of personal failure, or she might consider her feelings to be her own business, not anyone else's, or she might feel embarrassed to talk about such emotions, especially to a stranger. The sensitive social worker, tuned in to the feeling levels of this particular person, quickly became aware of the situation and was able to deal with it appropriately.

Even though the presenting problem may be different from the *real* problem, it is nevertheless significant to the consumer. As a defense, the presenting problem must be respected. It takes the worker's skill and usually time to establish a certain amount of trust before the person can move toward a more open and sharing attitude. If the consumer cannot move beyond the presenting problem, for whatever reason, the social worker must rcognize this block and deal with it with the utmost caution, treating the defensive verbalizations with as much respect as if the consumer had confessed all. The social worker must start where the consumer is "at," not where the social worker thinks the consumer ought to be. Inexperienced workers, eager to impress consumers with their skills, often tend to move too quickly, and even erroneously, intruding on areas that the consumer is not willing or even able to deal with. Such intrusive actions are incorrect, even if the interpretations are correct, for the social worker is violating the life-space of another human being.

Why Now? In considering the presenting problem, an important question to ask is, "Why now?" Why is *this* particular person seeking help with *this* particular problem at *this* particular time? Why a consumer requests service at a particular time may be related to the nature of the problem.

In dealing with an emergency or crisis situation, the answer is usually obvious. The loss of a job, an eviction notice—any event for which consumers have no ready answer may force them to seek help. In this respect, the "why now" question often contains the solution.

The "why now" question may also suggest an important clue to an underlying situation not revealed by the presenting problem, for what may appear on the surface to be a minor problem may mask an underlying problem of some complexity. If the situation being presented is long standing and no discernible recent event transpired to alter the situation, it can be surmised that the underlying problem is causing the distress in a manner necessitating immediate remedy.

The "why now" question invites responses that indicate the course of the work to some extent. When asked either implicitly (to oneself) or explicitly (to the consumer) it often provides a basis for a rapid but *preliminary* assessment. Although subsequent events and information may radically alter the assessment, it can nevertheless serve as a guide to determine whether the situation will be short or long term, and whether it will involve intervention in the environment (helping the consumer find a new job), in the family (helping the consumer deal with marital difficulties), or in the personality (helping the consumer deal with attitudes, emotions).

The "why now" question, however, does not ordinarily pertain to the consumer in an involuntary situation, such as a correctional institution or a state hospital, who is usually required to participate in interventionist procedures and only rarely seeks service voluntarily.

Where appropriate, the "why now" question is a preliminary step in preparation for the ongoing work with the consumer and, of course, must be reexamined in light of the ongoing work.

The Assessment. An "excellent" intake process includes an initial assessment that describes the nature of the situation, the consumer's strengths and limitations, the degree of priority that should be accorded to the case, and the next steps to be considered in the process.

That the consumer has voluntarily sought help from the agency is considered a sign of strength, regardless of the severity of the presenting problem. The consumer's recognition of a need for help is a healthy sign that bodes well for future work. People who cannot recognize their need for help or who are unable to ask for help are in a more difficult situation, which requires special skills from the social worker. But the consumer who recognizes his need for help and searches it out indicates a desire for change of some sort in his life. If the social worker can respond to this request for change by offering a means to change, a successful engagement may occur.

The intake process can also indicate the consumer's level of functioning. His activities and involvement are the clues. An employed family man involved in community affairs has a different level of functioning than a single, unemployed person, living alone. The former's level of functioning indicates strengths in the socially defined value sense, whereas the latter's level of functioning is more limited.

Fewer resources are available to the jobless single person, living alone: no immediately available family, no satisfaction from work performance, less peer support, less demonstrated capacity for independent functioning. It should be noted that the functioning level of a consumer does not correlate with his inherent worth.

The age of a consumer often relates to the problems encountered. The social worker's knowledge of the developmental stages of man and normative behavior at those stages may be directly applied. Are the consumer's activities appropriate to his age? Behavior suitable for an adolescent is often not appropriate for persons in their middle forties.

Even if the agency is not directly concerned with health, the consumer's health is nevertheless an important factor in assessing strengths and liabilities and in anticipating patterns of future work.

An assessment of the consumer's emotional health indicates

the extent of his relatedness to the world. Although the intake assessment is considered quite tentative, and may be cast aside during subsequent work, it can at least offer a guide in planning future roles and courses of action.

The religion or nonreligion of a consumer can indicate his value orientation. A consumer's religion and his church activities identify his potential resources.

Social class and income are also indications of the potential involvement of a consumer. A "delinquent" act committed by a teenager from an affluent family in an upper-middle-class neighborhood has a different import than the same act committed by a teen-ager from a ghetto. A gross assessment based on intake data leads to different conclusions even though the events are similar. For the ghetto teen-ager, the delinquent act may be attributed to ghetto survival, peer influence, or rebellion against injustice, and potential involvement, consequently, may move toward environmental manipulation and the introduction of alternate life-styles. For the upper-middle-class boy, such behavior may be indicative of intrapsychic problems and lead to intervention along therapeutic lines, such as personal or family counseling. Again, however, the initial assessment based on intake material may be reversed after further study.

In the beginning of any new case situation, a large amount of deductive reasoning takes place. Based on the evidence, what can the worker conclude? Based upon the information, what inferences can be made? There is a Holmesian quality to assessment, the mystery is pursued and more evidence is uncovered. For the social worker, in what system does the difficulty lie? Is it in the individual system, the family system, the environmental system? When the system is identified and the consumer and the agency agree, intervention can take place.

The "better" the intake, the more comprehensive and accurate it is, the better it sets the stage for the subsequent drama. But like any preliminary assessment, it can easily be replaced by new information or by a more reasoned interpretation of the old information. Although it does provide a framework for a subsequent course of action, there is nothing inherently precious about it. The danger is that the preliminary assessment often becomes a demonstration of the worker's professional skills, that new information is introduced in a manner calculated to prove the assumptions of the assessment rather than to achieve clarity in a given piece of work, an example of personal worker needs taking precedence over consumer needs. During actual work with the consumer, difficulties often arise to inhibit progress. Frequently it is the worker's need for prestige and control that has interfered with progress. Once identified, such impediments are easily rectified.

Accuracy is not essential to the initial assessment. An assessment serves only to temporarily frame a consumer in the worker's world in order to help. Because it is usually easier to work from a set of assumptions, a framework, than from chaos, assessments are designed to serve the consumer in the long run and the worker in the short run. They are not to be used rigidly, but flexibly, as possibilities. They serve as a stepping-off place and are subject to change with the addition of new information and new insights. Ultimately, the worker assigned to the case makes a more detailed assessment and develops interventionist strategies.

Assessments are not required in all agencies. But when the intake process is lengthy, involving many appointments and meetings, the intake assessment becomes increasingly important.

Permission to Act. Permission from the agency that mandates the work is necessary before social workers can act on the assumptions derived from the assessment. In a public-assistance agency the worker is primarily authorized to provide an economic function. If, in the course of determining and verifying an economic need, other problems arise, say, for example, a sexual problem, the consumer would probably be referred elsewhere.

In a private agency, however, a series of in-depth psychotherapeutic sessions might be provided if, of course, the problem was both appropriate to the agency and the consumer granted permission.

How to Read Intake and Permanent Records. The intake and case records establish the consumer's history at the agency—that is, what was done and how it was done—and what remains to be done. Inexperienced social workers are often overwhelmed by the amount of information in a permanent record or even in an intake report. It is not necessary to memorize the information. Records are there to serve the social worker, to supply the information needed to carry out assignments in the most efficient manner possible. When used properly, the record is a helpful tool.

The permanent record is a document of facts and evaluations concerning the consumer, his situation, how he is relating to the agency system, and how the agency system is relating to him. The record contains factual information, documented information, opinions, impressions, study material, assessments, correspondence, and so on, all of which is given relative weight when used. The confidential nature of the intake and the permanent record must be respected at all times. For the beginning worker, a quick "read" of the record to become familiar with the recording processes of the agency and to gain an initial impression of a case is helpful. As a recapitulation of agency experience with a particular consumer, a record can set up a frame of reference for a case situation, allow the worker to develop a preliminary "feel" for the consumer, and prepare him for his initial encounter. The record provides not only "background" but also the agency's work procedures and the aspects of the work that it chooses to emphasize.

Some records include *process recordings,* which are lengthy statements that recapitulate the interaction between the consumer and the social worker, an attempt to recapture in the written word everything that transpired in the verbal contact. For example: "I said 'hello.' Mr. X did not answer me but continued to read his newspaper. I then said . . " A process recording also contains expressions of feelings and attitudes on the part of the worker, often quite candid. The process recording often concludes with a summary statement that assesses the contact and includes plans for the next steps of the intervention. Process recordings not only inform the supervisor as to the progress of case activity, they also indicate skills that need improvement, such as interviewing and assessment techniques, and incidents of countertransference.

Process recordings often swell the size of the record itself to almost unmanageable proportions. For the new worker, an unwieldy record is indeed an awesome sight. Reading the process recording of another worker, however, offers valuable insights into practice and service delivery. A glance through the record establishes the general contours of the case, and closer attention to the more recent entries enables the new worker to become familiar with current events in the life of the consumer and thus anticipate more accurately the nature of the future contact.

THE ENCOUNTER

Subsequent to the intake interview and the determination that the consumer has indeed connected with the proper agency, a worker is assigned to the consumer and their first meeting, a "getting to know one another" meeting, is scheduled. Assuming the worker was not the intake interviewer, he is meeting the consumer for the first time, and although he has studied the intake record, the consumer may not appear to be exactly as the worker had anticipated. The worker's purpose here is to learn more about the situation that requires intervention and about the consumer himself, to present to the consumer an idea of the nature of the services, and to attempt to develop a possible course of action to accomplish the service. The consumer's purpose here is to assess how the help will be offered and the person who will do the helping. The goal is, of course, the development of a "contract," an agreement to carry out the mutual endeavor.

The social worker must assess the presenting problem—the situation as the consumer views it—in more detail than was possible in the intake interview. He must further refine the consumer's level of functioning—the resources available to him, such as family, job, stability, intelligence, and so on, or are his resources few, that is, is he vulnerable, alone, uneducated, jobless? If the consumer is well supplied with resources, the worker can proceed in one direction; if the consumer lacks resources, the worker may take a different direction and build more support and resources into the helping situation. In addition, the worker attempts to learn more about the range of available areas or systems where intervention may be considered, the beginning of an assessment process. These goals, which may require more than one contract to accomplish, are approached through a general framework that establishes a climate of understanding, acceptance, and interest, and offers a *realistic* possibility for change.

Establishing a Contract

Such terms as "rapport," "relationship," or even "helping" do not adequately describe the interaction between a social worker and a consumer. *Contract* may sound "commercial" rather than "professional," but the introduction of the term has forced the profession to examine with more precision the nature of the professional social work relationship and, consequently, has directed attention to the need for more specificity in the work. The word "contract" forces a focus on the specific help being given, how specifically it is being given, and for how long a time it will be given. By forcing attention to detail and the greater specificity that "contract" in the business sense demands, the term also forced a clarification of the professional role.

A contract is a definition of work; it identifies the work that a consumer system and a service delivery system are to do. A contract establishes the boundaries of service, identifying not only what *will be* accomplished but what *will not be* attempted; it establishes the conditions of work, the where and the when in addition to the how; a contract delineates the working responsibilities of both parties. By definition, contract implies mutuality, two parties working together under specific conditions to accomplish a mutual goal.

A contract is not necessarily a formal, written agreement, although some agencies may require one. Contracts are most often verbal agreements that include both issues that are negotiable and issues that are not negotiable, and like business contracts, the contract itself is frequently renegotiated. One step forward, two steps back, or new circumstances in the consumer's life may make an existing contract nonviable and call for a renegotiation. The importance of a contract does not necessarily lie in the details but in the fact that both parties, particularly the consumer, know that they are commited to an agreement.

All conditions of the contract should be discussed, of course, including non-negotiable items, which should be identified as non-negotiable at the outset. A social worker may have only a number of hours free and time cannot be offered beyond that. If a social worker has only Tuesday afternoons available, to negotiate over whether to meet on Monday, Tuesday, or Thursday would be not only inappropriate but arrogant and insulting. Presenting an illusion of choice to give a consumer something to work on or think about is a poor substitute for honest work. "I am only available on Tuesdays. How does that fit in with your schedule?" Contracts cannot be reached through pretense nor can effective work be carried out through illusion. A non-negotiable condition of a contract with a young boy may be that he cannot hit the social worker under any conditions; he may yell and scream, for example, but he cannot touch. Whether the social worker meets with the boy for fifteen minutes a day or an hour, however, may be mutually discussed and agreed to.

The art of contracting is usually as informal as, "Look, suppose we get together again next week at this time. I'll check out what you have to do to get unemployment insurance and you can check out the hotels to decide where you want to live, OK?" Contracts with sophisticated adults appear more formal; those with children appropriately on their level.

The conditions of the contract can be reviewed at any time, for clarity about roles and responsibilities is prerequisite for any successful service. With a contract that offers a clear statement of roles and assignments, the social worker is able to more carefully identify his purpose. When his focus becomes blurred in detail or over the course of time, a review of the contract can offer a refreshing step back and often another perspective on the work itself. When, however, during the subsequent weeks of the interaction, another problem, rather than the presenting problem, is uncovered, a basic renegotiation may be in order.

For example, a social worker in a public agency is working with an unemployed man in an attempt to help him find work in a tight job market. The consumer arrives to see the worker every Monday morning with a copy of the Sunday's want-ads. Together they look at the job opportunities and "role play" the job interview. They discuss the kind of clothes to wear to the interview, and the social worker provides money for the carfare. But then the consumer begins to talk about his fears of seeking work and relates them his feelings of sexual potency. The original contract called for specific responsibilities on both parties to effect change in an unemployment situation. It is now apparent, however, that an underlying problem must be dealt with first in order for the desired change to occur. To focus the work on the underlying sexual difficulties, the contract must be renegotiated. To initiate such renegotiation, a worker might say: "Look, it seems that there are other factors interfering with your finding a job. You seem to have a lot of concern about your sexual problems. Suppose for the next few weeks, instead of talking about job interviews, you tell me more about what's going on in that area of your life and perhaps I can be of some help." Before any new agreement could be concluded, there would be, of course, more discussion about the nature of the help and the role of the consumer.

Ideally, this renegotiation would be an appropriate way to handle this situation, but other considerations might prevent such a solution. As part of a service delivery system, the agency has a specific purpose. If the purpose of this agency does not include dealing with underlying personal problems, referral, of course, is indicated. The "contract" with this agency would be redefined, in essence, and the work would continue as defined; the "new" element would be dealt with elsewhere, if the consumer so decided.

When the conditions of the contract are not being met, when the consumer fails to show up, when the social worker fails to follow through, it is appropriate to ask, What is happening here? Why isn't the contract working? Is it unworkable? If adjustments or even a new contract cannot be agreed upon, work with the consumer is terminated. The contract should be flexible enough to deal with unforeseen factors of minor significance. Major events, however, such as illness, death, marriage, job loss, or fortune found, often require a major renegotiation.

Parts of or even the whole contract can be rejected by both the consumer and the agency on professional or other grounds. A potential consumer, whose child has a behavior problem, may approach an agency and say, "Tell her you will take her away or put her in jail if she doesn't behave." The agency can offer to work with the family within the professional context of the agency, but if the mother insists that the *only* working agreement she can tolerate is the one outlined above, the agency may be forced to deny a contract on that basis. Both sides must agree to the initial conditions of work. Following this basic agreement, some contractual items may be negotiated, but without initial agreement, no service can be rendered.

Reaching Out to Establish a Contract. For those consumers who need help but are resistant, hostile, or unmotivated, the social worker must *reach out* in an effort to establish a contract. Reaching out involves presenting one's services to those in need in a way that will attract a positive response. Salesmanship, perhaps, but not misrepresentation. For example, a simple identification of the services provided in certain circumstances will do the trick. The consumer was resistant because of his fear of the unknown.

Success in "reaching the hard to reach" is achieved when social workers believe in what they have to offer, when they believe that the services they perform are helpful and purposeful. A worker might say to a resistant consumer, "What seems to be the difficulty in getting involved? Why are you hesitant? Can we talk about that? It seems you don't trust me. What can I do to convince you that I am genuine? If we can start a dialogue, perhaps we can move toward a contract." By showing interest and concern, by offering professional help, the successful worker can reach the hard to reach. Reaching out, which is an attempt to reach a contract, involves the worker's expression of interest and concern for the person, a recognition of both the person as a human being and his place in the world.

With "captive" clients, as in a prison situation, where attendance is mandatory, the social worker must attempt to establish a contract that involves more than the mere presence of the consumer. Although mere presence may satisfy the rules of the institution, the worker must nevertheless try to help the consumer by at least showing concern, which is often an important communication to that consumer whether he responds to it or not.

With children or with mentally disturbed individuals, where verbal communication is difficult or impossible, a contract can be established by scheduled daily visits that in themselves indicate concern and sometimes even connection. When a social worker stops by every day at 10 A.M. to say "hello" to a catatonic patient, who, of course, cannot respond in the traditional way—perhaps by just a glance of recognition—the social worker is able by his routinized presence to communicate his concern. On this level the beginnings of a contractual agreement are in effect.

Attempts to establish a contract often involve the grinding work of unrewarding visits and hours spent in explanation of the service offered. When the resistance cannot be breached, when attempts to deal with the resistance have failed, the consumer's decision not to receive service must be recognized. Sometimes a small contract can be reached, a paltry, narrow focus over a brief time; but even this mutual agreement to work together is preferable to no contract at all.

Anxiety in the Initial Encounter

A beginning social worker, quite naturally, experiences some anxiety in his initial encounter with a consumer regardless of the effort involved in pre-encounter preparation. The anxiety merely indicates that the worker recognizes the importance of the encounter. Experienced workers as well experience anxiety when meeting a consumer for the first time, but usually on a lesser scale.

Initial anxiety overwhelms the new worker with its loudness. One worker put it this way: "An overriding sense of your complete and utter incompetence; you know absolutely nothing; you are about to be exposed as a fraud, a con person disguised as a social worker; you need more help than any consumer could possibly need; you would rather be selling fertilizer or become a business major." The self-doubt drowns out everything in its path. The worker, at that moment, can hear neither the sound of his own reason nor the ringing of the telephone nor the sounds of the consumer.

Although the above may be extreme for some, it is not uncommon for many. Factors other than the social worker's sensitivity are also involved. A brief "hello" to a ward patient does not usually cause great internal stress. If the initial contact is a prelude to extended work, however, there is more at risk and the anxiety thus increases. Status differentiation between the worker and the consumer also contributes to the anxiety level. The social worker usually finds it easier to work with someone who is younger or the same age, someone who earns less money, who has less education, who has a less important job. The consumer who is "superior" to the worker in any of the above ways poses a potential threat to the "control" needs of the social worker that usually results in a rise in the anxiety level.

The consumer, too, has his own set of anxieties about the situation that brought him to the agency, about his ability to fully share his needs and situation with the worker, about his own need to maintain "control" that has already been threatened to some extent by his act of seeking, and consequently admitting his need for, help. A consumer is often more concerned about how he is coming off in the worker's eyes than the other way around. Once social workers have recognized their own needs and concerns, they are able to recognize the needs and concerns of consumers.

The anxiety experienced by the beginning worker is usually not obvious in the encounter itself. Preoccupied with anxiety, the worker is often not fully aware of the many positive effects of the interaction. Although anxiety diminishes with experience and knowledge, it should not be allowed to escape completely, for it has an important positive role as well. In addition to indicating care and concern, anxiety serves as a defense against complacency; it forces the worker to be alert to the interactive quality of the contact and to his role within it, whereas unquestioned surety diminishes the potential of the interaction.

But if overwhelming anxiety continues, other factors should be considered, including the choice of social work as an occupation.

THE ONGOING INTERACTION

Interviewing Equals Interaction

The ongoing interaction is the procedure through which the consumer and the worker achieve their mutually agreed upon goals. Through the interviewing skills employed by the worker, an ongoing purposeful interaction between the two is developed and maintained. Almost everyone is interviewed at one time or other—for schools, for jobs, by the doctor, the lawyer, the teacher. As the main tool of the trade, however, interviewing is of prime importance to the social worker. In the "helping" encounter, successful interviewing does not result from the acquisition of techniques or tricks, but from the worker's conscious awareness of the interviewing process itself.

Purpose of the Interview. The purpose of the interview determines its form. In a crisis situation, for example, the primary purpose of the interview is to secure information relative to the crisis as rapidly as possible. If the consumer is upset, the worker attempts to calm him but at the same time get at the facts: "Try to tell me what happened." "When did you say it happened?" "Is that the first time?" "It sounds as though you had a rough time; what were you able to do about it?" The support offered by the worker allows the facts to surface, and from those facts she is able to make a preliminary assessment and determine the next steps to be taken. In crisis, unlike noncrisis, situations, interruptions are permissible for clarification purposes.

Conversely, in a noncrisis situation the gathering of facts is secondary. For example, sufficient information is already available on a clinic patient who is an outpatient from a state hospital when a new social worker meets him for the first time. The purpose of the interview is to allow the social worker to "get to know" the consumer and the consumer to "get to know" the worker. The primary purpose is to establish communication bridges between the consumer and the worker. "Hi, my name is . . . I'm your new social worker. Glad to get the chance to meet with you today . . . " The contact would be open, the questions usually open-ended. "Anything I can help you with . . . ?" Reaching out, the worker trys to get a sense of the consumer and to present his own interest and concern as well. "How are things going for you . . . ?" "Do you enjoy the program here . . . ?" Questions that convey concern, that are not perfunctory, that are asked with a seriousness of intent in an attempt to communicate to the consumer a genuine interest in his or her well-being. In this type of situation, the interviewer is usually active, inviting response and connection. Once the connection is made, the social worker tends to be less directive, is less apt to interrupt.

In an ongoing situation where relationship and contract have already been established, the purpose of the interview is to maintain the relationship and forge ahead in the area of problem solving. Rather than initiate communication, the social worker tends more to respond to the consumer's direction, allowing him to focus on the difficulties he is experiencing in, for example, finding a job or dealing with painful emotional feelings.

The Agenda of the Interview. Although the general direction of the interview is limited by its purpose and is determined by the worker, the agenda for the interview—its specific content and sequence—is determined by the consumer.

Inexperienced social workers are apt to carefully lay out an agenda, especially for first encounters, so that awkward pauses and silences can be avoided. Such interviews are often stilted— the interviewer asking questions, the consumer responding, first one, then the other—and the consumer often feels trapped, with little or no control over the content of the interview or the resolution of his situation.

Rather, the interview should be a flowing, dynamic interaction that allows the agenda to develop, as far as possible, from the consumer's, not the worker's, priorities. The worker's opening questions—''What's happening?'' ''How are you?''—are designed not only as questions to solicit information but as statements that, in turn, inform the consumer that the determination of the subject of the interview is up to him. When the consumer fails to honor the agreed-upon contract, or avoids dealing with difficult issues, the worker, of course, intervenes, but, in essence, the consumer produces the content and its sequence during the ongoing work. Any items deemed necessary by the worker should be introduced during natural breaks in the interview, at the end of the interview, or, where appropriate, during the exploration of the consumer's agenda, in which case the consumer can be helped to elaborate on them.

When inexperienced workers substitute form for flow,

"How would you briefly sum up your problem?"
"What resources do you have available?"
"Have you contacted friends and relatives for help?"

alienation often results, whereas,

"Suppose you tell me why you have come here . . . ?"
"You haven't paid your rent yet?"
"How have you tried to get it?"

elicits the necessary information in the context of the consumer's agenda. When the worker listens, rather than questions, the information is supplied with affect, with emotional content, and subsequently becomes more meaningful. "My parents are on welfare . . ." the consumer says—bitterly? matter-of-factly? arrogantly? casually? The consumer's relationship with his parents is thus revealed, whereas an automatic question, "Are your parents on welfare?" produces an automatic answer—"Yes." Working from the consumer's agenda also allows the flow of seemingly unimportant information that may open up areas for additional work in the future. Most important, the consumer who feels that he is really being listened to is able to allow the establishment of trust, from which beginning a valuable working relationship can be developed.

The Hidden Agenda. When a social worker says, "I'm helping Mr. Harris to separate from his wife," and the contract between them actually calls for family counseling, the concept of the "hidden agenda" is involved. The intention of a hidden agenda is not malicious but efficacious. In such situations, the worker is perhaps a half dozen steps ahead of the consumer.

The agenda is hidden, because the consumer will not agree to its content, at least not at this point in the relationship. But the consumer is nevertheless being manipulated toward an end about which he is uninformed. The hidden agenda is a denial of the process of work between the consumer and the social worker and implies, most significantly, a deception in the professional relationship that is guaranteed to destroy any accretion of trust. In its most gross form, the hidden agenda represents an unprofessional abuse of power and circumstance. In its more benign form, it avoids having to endlessly debate self-evident conclusions.

But to be effective, the work must include the full participation of the consumer. Far better to say, "Mr. Harris, there are two paths to follow here—either your troubles with your wife can be worked out or it might be best to go your separate ways." The consumer may not be ready for the latter alternative, but at least the door to the possibility of such a resolution has been opened, otherwise, the consumer's eventual recognition of the pain of deception is often more bitter than the pain of reality.

Effective Interviewing

"To thine own self be true" is a cardinal rule of interviewing as well as all other professional interactions, for only when the worker is comfortable with himself, with what he is saying and doing, will the message of interest and concern be conveyed to the consumer.

An open, spontaneous, outgoing, talkative social worker, given to gestures, should not attempt to be reserved, nor should a withdrawn, quiet, reserved worker attempt to be a chatterbox. To be false to oneself is to be false to the consumer and can easily communicate an insincerity that, despite skills and knowledge, often causes a consumer to be unnecessarily cautious. Honesty and sincerity will out, and, it is hoped, the consumer will respond in kind. When a worker is being himself he is honestly there, so to speak, not for himself but for the consumer.

Social workers, impressed by the success of other workers,

often try to emulate them. A young teen-age addict, very much into himself, sat in sullen silence, glowering hostilely and refusing to communicate with the new social worker. Struggling with the problem, the new worker recalled another time and another place and another social worker who had worked very effectively with young addicts in a drug treatment agency. Big and fat, the worker had been a street kid himself and was personally experienced with the drug scene. He was loud and aggressive, abrasive at times, outgoing, his language peppered with street slang. His professional technique included a combination of name-calling, mock threats, cajoling, and cursing. And it worked! Now, faced with the silent teen-ager, the new social worker wondered whether he should take off his tie, roll up his sleeves, and curse the hostile boy into communicating.

"Posing" as a social worker, adapting a "stance," or putting on a professional "demeanor" that can be turned on and off like a water tap belongs in the acting profession not in social work. "Acting" the part in a profession concerned with "unmasking" would, of course, be contrary to the basic principles involved. In addition, such deceptions are picked up very easily by the consumer. Regardless of the nature of the problem, the consumer is quite aware of the person to whom he is entrusting it. Pretense, phoniness, and even the stereotypical responses to which all social workers are prey can turn off a consumer before the first hand-shake is ended. The most successful workers are those whose approach is genuine. A worker who is himself, who makes no pretense, establishes, at the very least, an accepting, helping climate where work can proceed.

Self-awareness and self-control allow all the energies, thoughts, and feelings of the skilled interviewer to focus on the consumer. Again, the social worker's purpose is to serve the consumer's needs, *not* his own.

By understanding his own needs and being able to put them

aside in the interviewing situation, the worker can allow all matters being discussed to reflect either the consumer's needs or the appropriate change to be effected in the consumer's needs. The interviewer's questions and responses, predicated on the consumer's situation, are to serve the consumer, to help him look at himself and the world from a more self-fulfilling perspective, to help him to achieve his goals.

Successful interviews are obtained only after long experience and with the counsel of a skilled supervisor. When that pinnacle is reached and the self is successfully put aside and all the social worker's energies are consumer oriented, an almost egoless state occurs in the social worker. The self, in effect, is suspended when the total worker is involved in the struggles of the consumer. The "world" returns to the social worker—sounds reappear, self-concerns reemerge, and the business of individual living resumes—only after the consumer leaves. The work with the consumer is recalled as an intense objective interaction.

Empathy—understanding the world from the consumer's point of view, trying to imagine how he feels—allows the worker to "tune in" to the consumer and, through comments and questions, to reflect a sensitivity to what he is experiencing. True empathy equals true understanding—both escape the worker who is not totally involved.

To achieve empathy, that is, to be where the consumer is at in relation to thoughts and feelings, the worker's comments and questions must reflect the situation of the consumer. Such a seemingly innocuous question as "How are you?" is actually meant to determine where the consumer "is" so that the interviewer can "be with him."

"You seem upset today," the social worker says, after observing a consumer's distraught behavior. In attempting to be "with him" in terms of the noticed upset, the social worker is sending the message: "If you are upset tell me about it and we can deal with what's bothering you."

Being "with" the consumer does not mean being so far ahead that the worker is talking gibberish: "I see that you have a schizophrenic abreaction to environmental stress." Nor does being with the consumer mean being so far behind that the worker's questions are inane: "Where did you say you went after the dance last night?" in reply to an anguished consumer who asked, "Do you know what my mother just did to me?"

Being "with" the consumer means being with the consumer. It is necessary for successful interviewing. Being one *small step ahead,* however, means that the interviewer is engaged in the art of interviewing. By being one small step ahead, the worker is able to help the consumer make the next move. "Yes, I see what you mean . . . but . . ." The "but" is the one small step ahead, leading the consumer into thinking about his last statement.

> "Yes, I see that your wife is really making a lot of demands on you . . . but . . . what part do *you* play in the marriage problems you are having?" "Yes . . . but . . ." leads the consumer to the next step, which is to begin to look at himself in the problem situation.
>
> "Now that you have a job . . . have you thought about how to budget your money?"
>
> "What the teacher said upset you . . . but is there something more . . . you seem to be reacting very strongly to her criticism."

Because the problems at stake are not the worker's but the consumer's, the worker is able to maintain an objectivity that allows a clarity of vision. Because the worker can "see" ahead, he can lead the consumer to take that one small step ahead in the ongoing process.

In encouraging the consumer to take that step, to move ahead, the worker, of course, is risking error. However, because social work is not an exact science, a flexibility in approach is enjoyed by experienced social workers who are able to risk themselves in the interviewing situation. If it works, use it. A worker who uses the pragmatic approach must be willing to risk error, however, and be prepared to deal with errors as facts of professional life.

A worker sometimes finds himself *too far ahead* of the consumer. By observing signals from the consumer—blankness, doubt, skepticism, an inability to follow—the alert worker knows when he has moved too far too fast. The social worker could have missed the boat altogether, of course, but it is usually his timing not his direction that is wrong. For one reason or another the consumer is not yet ready to deal with the material and is rejecting it. The consumer has signaled a halt. The experienced social worker responds to that signal appropriately. However, if the social worker is indeed on the right track, he has nevertheless enabled the consumer to look ahead, to consider, no matter how briefly, the next step in the work. Even if the social worker's suggestion is incorrect, it requires a quick look at what *might* be done. That quick look, in itself, is an engagement in the process of self-help—if not what the social worker is suggesting, then what? That the social worker's suggestion does not have to be correct in order to help reiterates the axiom that the art of social work lies in helping people become engaged in those processes that will enhance their own lives.

But at what point, in view of the importance of timing, should the consumer start moving ahead? A consumer in the midst of grief over the death of her husband cannot be "hurried" along. "Yes, you're very upset over your husband's death yesterday . . . but . . . are you . . . ?" The sensitive social worker recognizes the need for sorrow, for a time to grieve, and does not hurry along but "stays with" the consumer, empathizing, holding, even just *being*. Consumers need time to allow their feelings to be resolved. When in doubt, the wise worker "stays with" the consumer. The consumer will signal when he is ready to move on.

Judge not . . . Judges are judgmental. That is what they are trained for and paid for. *For the most part,* social workers evaluate to understand human behavior not to deem such behavior good or bad. The social worker can say that such and such acitvity *may* lead to such and such consequence—if a boy steals a car he may be arrested. But workers neither approve nor disapprove behavior because dignity and respect are due all human beings regardless of their behavior. Beginning social workers, however, often have difficulty in learning to judge not.

In interviewing, especially, judgmental qualities are often revealed in responses and questions to consumers. A tone of hostility, a frown, a worker's own values and feelings can activate a host of factors that might jeopardize the work in progress.

Inexperienced social workers are apt to "lecture": "Drinking again, Mrs. Jackson—shame, shame. Don't you know you are ruining your children's lives?" Or, "Sam, you stole another car. You know that's wrong. You're a bad boy, all right, no two ways about it." Or, "Remember, George, your marriage vows—'love and honor, cherish and obey.' You and Ellie better stop fooling around." Blatant, yes, but only to emphasize the need to be constantly alert to the more subtle judgments conveyed by the raised eyebrow, the tapping pencil, the curt good-bye. Not to judge, but to understand. To help the alcoholic understand why he drinks and to perhaps offer him other activities to meet his needs. Telling a consumer how distasteful he is, is not reaching out but "turning off." When the child understands more about himself and the acceptable choices in life, stealing cars will be recognized as an unfortunate choice. When the errant husband understands how he is contributing to his marital situation, he may also better understand his options and assume more control over the direction he would prefer his life to take. When consumers understand the common human needs that underlie human activity and the internal and external factors that determine human behavior, they are better able to develop a more realistic attitude toward and control over their own lives. Because social workers understand that human behavior is caused by environmental and emotional factors, they are able to suspend judgment of any particular act itself and to move beyond the act and focus instead on the causative factors. The child molester is helped by the worker's understanding of the forces that produced the problem, not by a rejection of him because of his problem. Accusing fingers do not offer a climate for possible change.

As social workers come to understand the common current in which mankind drifts—these are not the first rapists, bigots, thieves, and murderers in history, after all—a certain tolerance is bred. People bound by fetters that force them into universally condemned activities and are consequently ostracized by society are to be pitied not punished.

In the actual work situation, obviously, moral indignation is taboo. When a consumer senses a worker's negative feelings about his difficulties, the turn-off is automatic. The consumer vanishes into the problem when he hears, "How could you be so stupid as to play hooky from school!" Whereas, "It seems that something is bothering you about school . . ." allows the consumer and his problem to surface and be recognized.

Questions—and Answers

The Yes/No Bind. Once the worker climbs aboard the "yes"/ "no" merry-go-round it is extremely difficult to get off.

"Do you like to dance?"
"No."

"Do you like to skate?"
"Yes."

"Do you like school?"
"No."

The yes/no bind is easy to recognize. It usually occurs when the worker's interest strays from the consumer to himself. What am I going to say? What am I going to ask next? Do I need any more information? In the anxiety to secure "information" and "facts" for later study or to avoid the bugaboo of silence, the worker panics, in effect, and settles down for a ride on the carousel.

But the yes/no bind is equally easy to avoid by simply asking the right kind of questions, the open-ended questions. Not "Do you love your mother?" but "How do you feel about your mother?" "How are things getting along at home?" not "Are you still quarreling with your parents?"

The yes/no bind may also be provoked by the consumer as a defense to avoid involvement with the work at hand. It can best be answered by addressing that issue itself: "It seems to me that you are not into talking about that today—what seems to be the difficulty?"

More often than not, however, it is the social worker who got on the merry-go-round and the social worker who must get off.

Responding. Because the skilled interviewer is also listening with his third ear, his responses will not always be to the content of the material itself but to the feelings inherent in the content.

"You don't sound that happy with school . . ."
"You seem pleased that you got the job . . ."

"You don't sound too certain about what is going on at home . . ."
"You seem concerned . . ."
"How do you feel about that?"

The ability to recognize and respond to the feeling content comes with experience. The how and when to respond to feeling content is a matter of timing, and when the worker is "with" the consumer, that is, just one small step ahead, the appropriate time to intervene is usually obvious.

"Something is bothering you about that . . ."
"It's not always that easy to . . ."

At times the worker almost senses the struggle the consumer is experiencing, and just the right gesture toward the feeling content may allow an important breakthrough in the helping process. When the timing is off, and the consumer is not yet ready to deal with the feeling material, he will turn the movement down. Even so, the worker has pointed a direction for exploration by the consumer and when he is ready he will backtrack and pick up the thread. When he is able to look at some of the factors that motivate and determine his actions, he is actively participating in the helping process.

These feelings that are close to the surface but denied are patent barriers to successful human functioning. When a consumer feels "guilty" about accepting public assistance when such assistance is his only available means for survival, he must be allowed to deal with that feeling in order to function. The social worker reaches out for feelings when they are relevant, when it is helpful to the consumer to do so.

In dealing with feeling content, the worker's response need not always be verbal. A smile, a puzzled expression, a nod of agreement, a nod of empathy, a questioning look, even a silence is a response that often relates more effectively than words to the underlying content. An encouraging nod is often sufficient to help a consumer plunge more actively in the process. Again, both the words and the gestures must be the worker's own. Disguised or artificial interaction communicates only that the consumer too must be artificial. If the worker cannot expose himself, why should the consumer?

Concern with feeling content should not obscure manifest content. What a consumer is *saying* must be considered along with what he is *feeling,* for one without the other is patently meaningless.

Anticipating Feelings. "Oh, you *must* feel . . ." is not the same as "It *seems* that you feel . . ." More than a semantic difference, the former is based on the social worker's prejudice about feelings, the latter on an observation of the consumer's feelings.

"I found a job."
"Oh, how happy . . ."

"My mother died."
"Oh, how sad . . ."

"My wife is pregnant."
"Oh, what joy . . ."

The social worker is informing the consumer how he *should* feel, the implication being that this *must* feeling is what one ought to feel *if one is like other people.* Obviously, if the consumer does not feel this way there must be something wrong with him. Because the social worker, in many instances, is an authority figure to the consumer and the consumer wants the approval of the "authority," a statement of how one *should* feel assumes more significance than would the same expression from a friend.

When a worker responds with "you *must* feel . . ." he is sharing his *own* values, his own sense about how this would make *him* feel.

"You *seem* happy . . ." allows the consumer not to be and to share whatever he does feel. The consumer must feel that his feelings, regardless of how bizarre, are acceptable to the social worker. Without such acceptance, the trust that allows communication cannot be maintained.

Feelings, in any event, don't follow easily discernible paths; they are often mixed, confused, and contradictory. Why must the person feel *only* pleased when he finds a job? Does a person feel *only* sad when his mother dies? *Only* joyous if his wife is pregnant?

Beginning social workers often have difficulty with these reactions in professional situations. Extreme caution must always be exercised to respond to the consumer's world, *his* feelings, *his* value system, *his* perspective, *his* philosophy.

Self-serving Questions. Often rationalized under a cloak of good intentions—to find out the consumer's reality level, to determine the consumer's IQ—self-serving questions belong in educational or psychological testing situations where they may be absolutely appropriate. For the social worker, however, such questions only create an atmosphere of deception, of gamesmanship.

When a worker who knows that a child has just been suspended from school asks, "And how are things in school?" he is setting a "trap" to determine not only the honesty of the consumer but also the level of his own arrogance. If the child says, "Fine," and the worker snaps back with, "Then how come you are suspended?" the superiority implied—"Don't try to get away with anything with me; I know too much"—can only stifle communication. "I hear you're having trouble in school and were suspended—what's happening?" accepts the situation and invites response without condemnation. And more important, the consumer perceives the social worker as being "up-front," as leveling with him. And, again, it is only in a trusting environment that true work can be achieved.

TERMINATION

Termination signifies the conclusion of the contract, the ending of the professional work relationship. It is sometimes a difficult emotional process. If the encounter has been "successful," a sense of accomplishment and satisfaction is dominant; if the encounter has been less than "successful," at least there is greater understanding of the difficulties involved in the situation itself and why it did not work out. Even when the termination occurs as a result of a change in a situation—the social worker moves to another agency, the consumer to another town—it nevertheless represents a complicated bag of accomplishments and nonaccomplishments. To the naked eye, the accomplishments themselves are often not startling—a slight change in direction, for example, or of attitudes toward self, so slight, in fact, they are often not visible to others; and then again, the change may emerge only after a passage of time. Or the change may be more obvious but not fantastic—a new job, a new home, a visible improvement in the quality of living or in overt behavior. To the people involved, however, the change is quite vital.

The process of termination, as consciously executed by the social worker, is a necessity that is almost as important as the first contact and the establishment of a relationship, part and parcel of the social worker's professional responsibility to the consumer. Even if the termination is particularly difficult—the consumer terminates service in a rage—the necessity for a termination process must be recognized by the social worker. Although in this case it is a recognition of the right of the consumer to terminate, it is also an indication of the social worker's concern for the consumer and his professional responsibility to draw a conclusion to the work. To a large extent, the termination process is determined by the reality of the circumstances, but whatever the reality, it is the responsibility of the social worker to press the process to its fullest. In a planned situation, the termination may be introduced and worked on almost at leisure; in a sudden situation, the termination may, by necessity, be brief. The necessity of terminating with the consumer reflects a professional concern and a recognition of the dignity and self-determination capability of the consumer. The worker cares about the consumer and what happens to him and if future services should be needed, the door is always open.

The termination process is essentially a recapitulation of the work done together, a "summing up." The social worker recognizes and acknowledges to the consumer that the gains accomplished were principally the result of the consumer's efforts and abilities. The accomplishments reflect *his* strengths, not those of the social worker. The social worker has always served as the *enabler,* not the doer. It is essential that this message be made very clear to the consumer. The areas where no discernible gains were made must also be identified fully and the process examined for potential causes.

The summing up reviews both the initial purposes of the contract and the distance traveled to its conclusion. A recapitulation is particularly necessary when the working relationship has been an extended one. But even a brief relationship requires a summing up.

Generally, the termination process involves considerable feeling from both participants. The consumer, particularly if he has been actively engaged in the process, may feel frightened at the prospect of continuing without the social worker. Or he may feel exhilarated, or even angry. The social worker must recognize these feelings and deal with them appropriately.

If the working relationship has been brief and the contract focused on an area of concrete service, a simple acknowledgment of the consumer's feelings may be sufficient: "It's hard, sometimes, to end a working relationship such as this . . ." or "I've really enjoyed working with you, as I hope you have with me . . ."

If the relationship has been extended and the contract essentially therapeutic, the consumer's feelings toward the social worker should be acknowledged and dealt with as part of the treatment process in the same manner that other feelings were dealt with during the relationship. Sufficient time, insofar as is realistically possible, should be made available to the consumer for the expression of his feelings about the process, which can include a host of feelings, ranging from love to hate with all possible combinations in-between. Too often, feelings get blocked up and the consumer is only able to respond in clichés. A decision to pursue this aspect of the consumer depends on the specific situation. It may well be remembered that feelings are oftentimes better expressed nonverbally.

Many social workers feel that the termination process allows them the only opportunity they have to express their own feelings directly to the consumer. If those feelings are positive, well and good, but if they are negative, are they to be kept under wraps? Is the social worker's message to the consumer that it is permissible to express only positive feelings?

The best solution is to hew as closely as possible to the quality of the interaction of the preceding ongoing relationship. The terminal interaction is "work" oriented. Following a discussion of the consumer's feelings, the social worker concludes with a summing-up statement, an assessment, a review of accomplishments and nonaccomplishments, and remarks concerning the availability of various appropriate services that might be needed in the future.

The successful social work relationship provides the consumer with a climate of hope. As the relationship terminates, the hope is that the consumer is now in a better position to make the most of his life, with all its pleasures and vicissitudes, as a result of the professional contact.

Termination is often experienced by the worker as a sense of loss and a sense of pain. Now he must move on to another troubled human being. But there is always more help—and more hope—to be extended.

FOR FURTHER
READING

Austin, M., A. Skeling and P. Smith. *Delivering Human Services*. New York: Harper & Row, 1977.

Cumming, E., and J. Cumming. *Ego and Milieu*. New York: Atherton Press, 1962.

Ferguson, E. *Social Work, an Introduction*. New York: Lippincott, 1975.

Fink, A. E. *The Field of Social Work*. 7th ed. New York: Holt, Rinehart and Winston, 1975.

Garrett, A. *Interviewing, Its Principles and Methods*. New York: Family Serice Association of America, 1955.

Germain, C. F. "An Ecological Perspective in Casework Practice," *Social Casework*, June 1973.

Golan, N. *Treatment in Crisis Situations*. New York: Free Press, 1978.

Hamilton, G. *Theory and Practice of Social Casework*. New York: Columbia University Press, 1951.

Kahn, A. J. *Social Policy and Social Services*. New York: Random House, 1973.

Macarov, D. *The Design of Social Welfare*. New York: Holt, Rinehart and Winston, 1978.

May, R., E. Angel and H. F. Ellenberger. *Existence*. New York: Basic Books, 1961.

Meyer, C. H. *Social Work Practice*. 2nd ed., New York: Free Press, 1976.

Muller, H. J. *The Children of Frankenstein*. Bloomington: Indiana University Press, 1970.

Mumford, L. *The City in History*. New York: Harcourt, Brace & World, 1961.

Pincus, A., and A. Minahan, eds. *Social Work Practice: Model and Method*. Itasca, Ill.: F. E. Peacock, 1973.

Piven, F. F., and R. A. Cloward. *Regulating the Poor: The Function of Public Welfare*. New York: Pantheon Books, 1971.

Reik, T. *Listening With the Third Ear*. New York: Grove Press, 1948.

Reusch, J., and W. Kees. *Nonverbal Communication*. Berkeley and Los Angeles: University of California Press, 1956.

Richan, W., and A. Mendelsohn. *Social Work: The Unloved Profession*. New York: New Viewpoints, 1973.

Richmond, M. E. *Friendly Visiting Among the Poor*. New York: Macmillan, 1899.

Romanyshyn, J. M. *Social Welfare: Charity to Justice*. New York: Random House, 1971.

Schwartz, W., and Z. Serapio, eds. *The Practice of Group Work*. New York: Columbia University Press, 1971.

Sobey, F., ed. *Changing Roles in Social Work Practice*. Philadelphia: Temple University Press, 1977.

Towle, C. *Common Human Needs*. New York: American Association of Social Workers, 1952.

INDEX

ABOUT
THE AUTHOR

Allan R. Mendelsohn was born in Brooklyn and studied at Brooklyn College, the New School for Social Research, and New York University. A former professor of field work at Columbia University School of Social Work, where he continues to tutor and instruct, he is now engaged in the private practice of social work and is a social work consultant. He is the coauthor, with Willard C. Richan, of *Social Work: The Unloved Profession*, published by New Viewpoints in 1973.